LONGING
FOR
LOVE

RUTH SENTER

BETHANY HOUSE PUBLISHERS
MINNEAPOLIS, MINNESOTA 55438

7.99

Bethany House Books by Ruth Senter

Can I Afford Time for Friendships?
(with Stormie Omartian & Colleen Evans)

Have We Really Come a Long Way?

Longing for Love

9612

LONGING
FOR
LOVE

Longing for Love
Copyright © 1991, 1997
Ruth Senter

Illustrations by Patrick Welsh

Originally published by NavPress, Colorado Springs, Colorado

Published by Bethany House Publishers
A Ministry of Bethany Fellowship, Inc.
11300 Hampshire Avenue South
Minneapolis, Minnesota 55438

Printed in the United States of America.

Library of Congress Cataloging-in-Publication Data

CIP Data applied for

ISBN 1–55661–939–1   CIP

RUTH SENTER is the author of eight books. The former editor of *Partnership* magazine and contributing editor to several Christian magazines, she is an active speaker. Ruth has a B.A. in communications from the University of Illinois and an M.A. in journalism from the Wheaton Graduate School. She and her husband, Mark, live in the Chicago area.

CONTENTS

He has taken me to the banquet hall,
and his banner over me is love.
Song of Songs 2:4

PREFACE

———————— ❧ ————————

I walk tonight into the semi-darkness of a church sanctuary. Mechanically, I reach for the hymnal in front of me. The man on the platform has another suggestion. We stand and begin to sing from memory "Jesus loves me this I know. . . ."

The words are so familiar I don't even have to think about what I'm singing. But tonight, for some divine reason, I do. The simple truth contained in the song of my childhood goes to my heart, like an arrow driven straight. I am quieted. Hushed. Humbled. Awed. Silenced, except for the song.

"Jesus loves me this I know." What else do I need to know? What else do I need to feel?

"Jesus loves *me*." What would happen if I really believed this? How would I be different? What would happen if I woke up every morning with the thought, *I am loved*? What if I moved through my day, ate my lunch, wrote my articles, read the paper, cooked dinner, with the thought *I am loved* always in the front of my mind? How would I respond to my children, greet my neighbors, treat my fellow employees, negotiate with the auto mechanic, if I truly lived with a sense of God's love and delight?

Our voices die against the vaulted ceiling of the church sanctuary. The song ends. My journey begins. It is as though God Himself has sung right through the rafters, rode in on the organ pipes, and whispered ever so softly into my ear, "I love you, Ruth. Stop trying so hard to do love. Let Me teach you what it means to be loved."

What does it mean? I do not yet know, but I am ready to start learning.

Come, then, and take the journey with me.

PROLOGUE
When Love Ran Dry

───────────── ❦ ─────────────

Once upon a time there was a woman who lost her sense of being loved.

She had been created for the Garden she forgot. God had formed her to breathe His breath of life, commune with His holiness, cultivate His creation, enjoy His love forever. She was made to walk with Him in the cool of the day, relax in His presence in complete transparency before His gaze.

Once upon a time, she had nothing to fear. The plan was for her to know the security of His love. In Eden, there was no reason to doubt. In Eden, she did not have to ask for evidence of His love. She simply took His word, received His delight in her.

In Eden, she did not have to prove her worth. She simply knew her worth. He loved her, didn't He? In Eden, she didn't need to understand His love, she simply opened wide her arms to it. She was forever in His heart and mind. Hers was the simple joy of knowing she was loved.

But today she is a long way from Eden as she zooms down the expressway, glancing frantically from her watch to her rear-view mirror to the speed-limit signs that remind her she is going faster than her limits.

She is on her way somewhere — always on her way somewhere. Giving love. Doing love. Modeling love. Being love. Working hard at love. Bible studies. Bible classes. Church visitation. Home visitation. "Meaningful" coffees. "Meaningful" lunches. Seminars. Retreats. Conferences. Outreach. Inreach. Around-the-world reach. . . .

"Excuse me, Lord, if I speed just this once. I have to get there, and I *have* to be on time. . . ."

She always has to be on time — for someone else's sake. She must get there on time to hold their world together — to hold *her* world together. To be organized, efficient, and in control. To do the work of loving. To meet expectations. She can't afford to let someone down by being late.

Who is she letting down if she's late? She never stops to ask the question. She knows only that she must meet the specifications. She must do the work. *Loving. Serving. Giving. Being on time.* Forever concentrating on the love she must give rather than on the love she has been given.

It is the way she runs her world. She is today's modern woman. God has blessed her with systems for doing love. Day-Timer personal planners. Seven-Star Diary organizers. Desk-top calendars, purse calendars, hanging-on-the-wall calendars. Three-ring binders with plastic strip dividers.

Files for addresses, recipes, favorite quotes, days of the week, rooms of the house, books of the Bible, seasons of the year, next year's long-range plans, last year's short-term evaluations. She tries to keep the systems well oiled. Grease the wheels of productivity. A place for everything, and everything in its place. Punctual. Precise. Efficient, but void of spirit, lacking heart, out of tune.

Out of tune? Certainly not with all the loving things she's doing. Such acts of love call for acute tuned-in-ness. Tuned in to God, to herself, to others. Neat little three-point outlines. She's given them often. She is always thinking outlines. How else will she pass on her insights about love? Her transitions must be clear. Her words must flow. Otherwise, how will she inspire others to love?

But the One who knows her best knows that she is a song without melody, a well without water. There is no spirit to her day, only schedule. No heart, only habit. No sense of wonder or quiet contemplation, only compulsion to work. (For how will she know when she has given enough love?) No messages of love direct from the One who loves her most, only noise and clamor and someone else's thoughts about love.

Where is God's voice? Buried beneath the clutter of voices that make her wise. If she is to do love, she must attend lectures, read books, sign up for seminars. She must know how to do it. She must be able to tell others how to do it. She must become an expert at loving. That's what she's after—although, of course, she would never say it in so many words.

Before long, being known as a loving person

becomes her god. Godliness is sacrificed at the altar of reputation, until she can no longer tell love for the sake of reputation from love for the sake of love. No one really knows for sure.

Except the One who knows her best and loves her most. There are no games with Him. He knows her love charades. And eventually others will, too. Hollow people fall quickly. Form without substance soon blows away like chaff in the wind. And the Master of love Himself cries out at the empty performances: "Stop bringing meaningless offerings! . . . You [have become] like an oak with fading leaves, like a garden without water."[1]

So one day, love ran dry. The woman who forgot Eden, who had lost her sense of being loved by the God of the universe, who was so busy giving love, found to her dismay that she had nothing more to give. One does not give what one has not received. Is a well without water still a well? Is an apple tree without apples still an apple tree? Can a song without melody still be a song?

She had lost her sense of being loved. She had lost her ability to give love. She was spent. Hollow. Dry. Mechanical.

Until the Master walked through the garden in the cool of the day and called, "Where are you?"

The modern woman answered in a still, small voice, ". . . here I am."

"Come," He said.

So she brought herself to Him—without calendars, without agendas, without lists or outlines, long-range plans, or evaluation forms. She simply brought herself.

And God smiled. "Finally, now we can talk. . . ."

And once she started talking, she found out how much she had to tell Him. He listened patiently, without judgment or pronouncement. When He answered, His words were gentle.

Here, then, is what they said. . . .

NOTE
1. Isaiah 1:13,30.

1

I AM NOT WORTHY
The Longing for Approval

———— ❦ ————

nce upon a time, Lord—long ago—things were perfect. Everything You created was good enough. The food was good enough. The weather was good enough. Relationships were good enough. *I* was good enough.

I never even thought to wonder about "good enough"—whether I was doing it right, whether You would stop loving me if I did it wrong. I did not worry about failure, agonize over shortcomings, fear mistakes.

You would come into Eden toward the cool of evening, and I would run to greet You with outstretched arms. I welcomed Your love, took it to my heart as naturally as a child takes to a mother's breast.

I was not afraid of love, then. It did not remind me of all I was not, but rather of all I was. I did not have to apologize—"Thanks Father for putting up with me." There was no doubt in my mind that You enjoyed me. I did not run from Your penetrating gaze, for I had nothing to hide. I was not ashamed so I had no need for cover-ups. No need to impress, to make myself look better, to live up to the standard, to compare myself with anyone else.

You had declared me "good," even as You sculpted me, stood me upright, and called me by name. "It is good," You said. "What I have called clean, let no one call unclean."

But I did. I called myself unclean because I *was*. I tasted forbidden fruit. I made a wrong choice—a choice I thought would make me look better than good. I was already perfect, but I thought I could improve perfection. After that, I ran and hid my face from You, behind the very trees that had once sheltered pure love.

From then on, the welcoming path was empty. I didn't eagerly move toward You anymore, only away from You.

You had created me perfect, to live in a perfect world with other perfect people. In Your garden, I gave and received perfect love. No strings attached, no conditions, no doubts. I drank deeply of Your love and was satisfied—never disappointed.

But Lord, Your creation creaked and groaned beneath its own weight. I creaked and groaned and disobeyed. Perfect love was forever spoiled, tainted by my self-centeredness. Loving became self-conscious. Effort set in.

Today I am a long way from home. But I have not forgotten Eden. You have banished me from it for a while; still every day, it seems, I knock at its gates, trying to recreate perfection, calling to myself for perfect love, pure sacrifice, uncontaminated zeal. I park just outside, unload the moving van as though I might move back into eternal spring, where the azaleas always bloom and the lilacs always fill the air with the fragrance of pure love, joy, peace, long-suffering, gentleness, goodness, faith. But the gates to Eden never open, no matter how hard I attempt to repossess. I no longer live there. I cannot return.

Lord, it would be so much easier to love if I still lived in Eden, if I were still a child of Your garden. Then I could accept Your love as a statement of truth and not some proposition to be tested. When You said, "I love you," I would never say, "Prove it." When You said, "This is the best way," I would follow without checking my road map. When You said,

"Here's My gift to you," I would not ask what it was before I opened it. When You gave, I would take. When You spoke, I would not doubt. Ours would be love, pure and simple — perfect both in the giving and in the receiving.

I know, dear Lord, that Eden was another time, another place. Paradise is lost. But still sometimes when I come to You, I feel I must come through the garden first, as though I must dress up for You in order to be presentable. You are a God of perfect love; You deserve to have perfect love stand before You. You are kind; I cannot bring my harshness to You. You think positively of all Your creation; I cannot bring to You my negative critiques. You are the silence of perfect strength; I can't come yakking my way into Your presence, going on and on about all the things I'd like to be but am not.

Such pure love as Yours deserves purity in return. If You love me wholly, I should love You wholly. If You love me unconditionally, I should love You unconditionally. Lofty love should draw forth lofty love. When a gift is given, shouldn't one of comparable measure be returned? I must give a worthy gift.

But standing next to greatness reminds me of my weaknesses; next to pure love, of my impurities; next to patience, of my impatience. And I go away sorry that I have nothing better to offer You, especially when I think of all You are. I forget about the rich man who went away sorrowful because he had *too much* to offer You.[1]

Should I not bring to You the firstborn of my flock — the best of my offerings? Will it not please You even as You looked with favor on Abel and his offering rather than on Cain who brought You less than best? When I feel my offering might not be acceptable to You, I join Cain in running from You rather than to You.[2] I apologize, defend, withdraw, or lament with great pity on myself that I am such a failure in my attempts to be more loving.

Lord, I am burdened by my endless wondering about acceptable sacrifices, by my harsh critiques of myself. I perform the routine without even thinking: "Check one: Always loving enough; sometimes loving enough; never loving enough." I mentally punish or reward myself depending on how I think I've done for the day, like crediting a child for whether or not she brushed her teeth. Gold stars for good days, blank spaces for bad. Maybe I project that You do the same: Reward when I deserve it; withhold when I don't. "Act lovingly and I will love you. Make yourself beautiful and you can join my club. Organize your life and you get to play on my team."

Your love is above the human games we play. But still I try to *deserve* Your affection—as though You might change Your mind about loving me if You find out what I'm really like. Human love withdraws when expectations aren't met; perhaps this is what I fear. If I'm not worthy, Your love will be transferred to someone worthier. Someone prettier. Wittier. Smarter. More loving. More patient. More self-sacrificing.

It is a terrifying thought, this fear of losing love because I don't measure up. I am forever a child, looking up at You, my heavenly Father, constantly asking You, "How am I doing? What do You think of me now?"

It is heavy, this self-imposed standard of worthiness I carry around. I feel it today, even as I join worshipers here in this black church on the city's west side. I am here more out of obligation than desire. I do not feel particularly loved today, from sources either human or divine. In fact, about all I feel is the plastic back of the chair sticking to my blouse in a bond of sweat, and the hot August air that circulates mildly around me when the oscillating fan moves in my direction.

I am self-conscious sitting here in the second row of this gymnasium-turned-church. The only things standing between me and the podium are a row of chairs and a communion table, on which sit an open Bible, red silk flowers arranged in a plastic vase, and a forgotten pair of sunglasses. I do not know the words to the songs, and I am awkwardly aware that I am swaying left when the rest of the congregation is swaying right. I have never jumped for joy before and though the words call for a purposeful jump of praise I am glued to the floor.

I do not have the rhythm, the words, the feelings. I am not into the black experience. I am not into the worship experience. I am not into much except myself. No wonder I have not thought about being loved. If I am so full of myself, how can I know that someone loves me?

The beat goes on. The sermon goes on. Two hours and thirty minutes go by. My stomach rumbles in protest—my only consolation is that no one hears it. The concluding soloist has concluded for the fifth time. Finally, the choir marches to the risers to sing the benediction. Little do I realize they will be singing to me.

But they do. They sing right through my pre-occupation with myself. Right through my "How am I doing, Lord?" Right through my lofty standards of perfection for myself. Right through all the wearisome "should be's" I have heaped up for myself in order to deserve Your love. Right through all the fancy dressings I put on when I come to Your dinner table. The organ wails. The drums beat. But I hear the words. *This time I hear the words:*

> *I'm Yours, Lord.*
> *Everything I've got.*
> *Everything I am.*
> *Everything I'm not.*
> *I'm Yours, Lord!*
> *Try me now and see*
> *See if I can be,*
> *Completely Yours!*

And through the sounds of this hot August afternoon, blasted in on snare and kettle drum, it's as if I hear His voice. . . .

You don't have to be anything for Me except what you are, My child. *You are Mine.* Everything you are *and* everything you are not. Give Me your best, yes, but don't stop there. Give Me your worst as well. I am big enough to handle both.

Relax, My child. You are loved just because you are. I am the One who knows you best and also the One who loves you most. You were loved from eternity past, even before I brought you to life in your mother's womb. "All the days ordained for [you] were written in [My] book before one of them came to be."[3] You will be loved until eternity future when I will carry you across the threshold of the New Jerusalem, as My bride. I will wipe away your tears, and we will sit down to dinner, and you won't have to worry about what you are wearing. You will take freely of My love and we will be together, home at last.[4]

So hand over all those long lists of "I should be's." You should be Mine. That is enough. You *are* Mine. That is enough! I didn't create you to be perfect, I created you to be My own.

This means you can put aside those high and lofty standards for yourself. Only one Person met those standards: My only Son, Jesus Christ. You are not perfect, but He is. When I look at you, you are wearing His perfection—His righteous robes. So stop worrying about all you are not. Relax in all My Son is for you. I can bear your imperfections because I see Him in you, even as a parent is imaged in a newborn.

And as for Eden, don't try to recreate it. Perfection was intended for the garden, but I closed its gates long ago. Boarded it up and sealed it away until another day, another time. You must recall Paradise now and then to be reminded of holiness, but you get yourself into trouble when you pretend you still live there.

Remember you are part of a flawed world. This is what My love is all about—to love you in your flawed condition. Because I am rich in love, I made you alive while you were still dead.[5] Some people will die for good people. I died for you *before* you were good—while you were still a sinner.[6] It was not My way to ask you to be loving before I could love you. And it is not My way to ask you to be loving in order for Me to continue loving you. Your world makes promises based on how well you respond. I love you regardless of your response. Your world changes people, then loves them. I love you first, and along the way, because you are loved, you are changed.

So take your mind off yourself. It is the trademark of lovers to gaze not inwardly at themselves but outwardly toward each other. As you focus on Me, you will wonder at My love rather than worry about your own. You will be so busy learning about Me that you won't have time to ask how you are doing. You will be so filled with a sense of My love for you that you will forget self-critiques. Love is what happens when you look away from yourself and toward another.

Stop trying to be perfect in order to deserve My love. You will never be "enough" of anything, anyway. I do not want your worth, your efforts, your gifts and credentials and produce. *I want you simply because you are you.* If tomorrow, you should become anything other than what you are today, still I would want you. If you were·in a horrible fire and burned beyond recognition, if you contracted a dread disease and became deaf and dumb, if you could not lift a finger to love anymore, still I would want you. My love is for *you,* not for what you are.

And I understand, My child, that you do not return perfect love. I know about this flawed creation of Mine. I did not will it to be flawed, but

I will allow it for a while. I must ask you to do the same — allow it awhile. It is part of My redemptive plan. You need not apologize, agonize, or pretend that brokenness does not exist. You were broken and I loved you. You are still not completely whole and still I love you. I have fixed you, redeemed you, but not perfected you. That will come later.

Someday you will be free from self-conscious love. But until then, you must accept your limitations. Until then, I will carry you where I want you to go, deeper into My heart of love. It is the only place you need to go. It will be the place of peace for you, for as you come close to My heart of love, you will forget about what you should be. You will also forget about what *others* should be. You will feel the beat of My heart in love for you. You will know you are loved; it will be all you need to know.

So do not strive for perfection. Rather, open yourself to My love. Fix your eyes on the deep, wide ocean that cannot contain My love for you. Look to the sky and know that from east to west you will not find the beginning or the ending of My love for you. Pore over the volumes of the ages and know that no one has ever been able to find enough words to describe My love for you.

Feel the ache of My heart as I dressed My Son in robes of righteousness and sent Him to your spinning orb so that He might be perfect in your place. Feel My pain over the nails that tore His flesh, My darkness over His call for help, which I could not answer. Feel My longing for My absentee Son whom I sent to you, and then you will know how great is My love for you. . . .

❦

I walk from the gymnasium-church in the heat of the day. The music is still wailing but the benediction has been pronounced. The service has moved into the post-service, but we have decided to find McDonalds. I do not worry that my fresh linen blouse is a mess of sweaty wrinkles, that my makeup has long since run with the heat, that there is still a streak of pink bubble gum along the side of my shoe from my walk between parking lot and front church steps. My hair is matted to my forehead, but I do not even try to fluff it out.

I am loved! I knew it once. When did I lose it in the shuffle?

I step toward the car with my head high, my back straight. Even the muggy world of this urban afternoon sings in praise. Never mind that the gutter is lined with soggy papers from yesterday's rain and that broken glass from a brown beer bottle litters the curb where I step. "I'm Yours, Lord, everything I've got. . . ." I open the door to my Pontiac 6000—in need of a tune-up. "Everything I am . . . everything I'm not . . . I'm Yours, Lord, try me now and see . . . see if I can be completely Yours!" I glance in the mirror at my soggy self. It is all okay. I come to You, dear Lord, just as I am. "Just as I am . . . Oh Lamb of God, I come, I come."

> *I came to You sad.*
> *You did not say, "Be happy."*
> *Instead,*
> *You cried with me;*
> *my tears rolled down Your cheeks*

29

so great was Your love/pain for me.
I did not have to be anything when I came to You
but me.

I came to You frazzled.
You did not say, "Be calm."
Instead,
You took my hand and said,
"Tell me about it. . . ."
I told You
and in the telling I was calmed.
I did not have to be anything when I came to You
but me.

I came to You absorbed in myself.
You did not say, "You're too introspective."
Instead,
You waited around
until I could reach beyond myself,
until I was released from myself.
I did not have to be anything when I came to You
but me.

I came to You just as I was.
You welcomed me into Your arms.
You gave me myself,
and the gift was priceless.

NOTES
1. Luke 18:18-30.
2. Genesis 4:2-7.
3. Psalm 139:13-16.
4. Revelation 21–22.
5. Ephesians 2:1-10.
6. Romans 5:6-8.

2
I CANNOT DO IT ALL
The Longing for Relief

or as long as I can remember I've worked hard at loving. It is what you, Lord, wanted me to do. It is what my parents, my Sunday school teacher, my youth leader, my college dean, my pastor, everyone wanted me to do.

It is still what You would have me do, still what people expect me to do—the loving, serving, self-sacrificing thing. It is what my faith is all about.

And so I take to the streets to work out my faith and to demonstrate my love. Services. Sessions. Committee meetings. Studying. Sharing. Listening. Baking. Calling. Running. Standing. Walking. After all, you've said that faith without works is dead. So it is with love, I suppose. Love without works is dead. If love doesn't work itself out, is it love at all?

Love one another. You said it again and again. Not just love each other, but "love each other as I have loved you." Your love was a working love. Always feeling the other's pain and placing Your hand at the point of hurt. Anticipating hunger, then filling baskets with the leftovers. Walking dusty roads to call forth life. Touching a blind spot and bringing sight. Calling the demon by name and creating calm. Yours was love on the move. Love in action. Love wrapped in deeds. Love that served. Love that gave until it died and resurrected to give again.

I must *do* love. It is the compulsion of faith. Without it, I become a self-contained knot, tied up with me. Eliminate loving service and I'm back to where the spiral downward began—preoccupation with self.

You had harsh words for those who live in self-containment—"If anyone does not provide for his relatives, and especially for his immediate family, he has denied the faith and is worse than an unbeliever."[1] You took drastic measures against those whose love stopped with themselves. You drove them from the garden.

Now I'm stuck trying to reverse the spiral downward. If I would find myself, I must give myself. If I would keep, I must lose. If I would receive, I must give.

Doing love is not only what You expect from me, it is also what needs to be done. The harvest is ripe. Laborers are few. . . . Night is coming, when no one can work.[2] So I must rise and shine, for the light has come. I must waken with the 5:30 alarm. The work is there. Dirty dishes all over the counter, soiled clothes stuffing the laundry shoot, two days' worth of *Chicago Tribune* spread over the couch. A Bible study that has no leader. A women's retreat that just lost its speaker.

Work, work, work. "Whatever your hand finds to do, do it with all your might."[3] "Heartily your hands should move in the service of His love, with unceasing labor true, both to saint and sinner too, till He comes, when you will be serving Him eternally." The admonition came in the mail with a clipping from a friend. I am spurred to do more.

My parents taught me industry. I prize it as gold. I covet it for my children. I must wash the dishes, do the laundry, pick up the newspapers, teach a Bible study. It needs to be done.

You like clean houses, don't You, Lord? You like well-run committee meetings and well-crafted Bible studies. You value work. It was part of the original garden plan. Name the animals. Tend the garden. Pull the weeds. Hard. Diligent. Conscientious work. Statement of our love for You. Statement of our love for others.

"Do I love you? I darn your socks and cook your meals and sweep your floors, don't I? Do I love you? Of course I do." Tevya's wife said it to him in *Fiddler on the Roof*. I have said it with different words.

Sometimes, dear Lord, it's as though work is the only language of love I know. As long as I'm doing what needs to be done, doing what You would have me do, doing what others think I should be doing, doing what is on the list, it is "true" love. It is also exhausted love.

Then, Lord, there is also the matter of the debt I owe. From everyone who has been given much, much will be demanded.[4] For You, loving me meant You gave everything. "What wondrous love is this, O my soul, O my soul! What wondrous love is this, O my soul! What wondrous love is this that caused the Lord of bliss to bear the dreadful curse for my soul, for my soul, to bear the dreadful curse for my soul."[5]

You loved me so much, You *did* something for me—walked the narrow, crowded streets of Jerusalem, carrying Your own weight of torture on Your back, enduring jest and ridicule, climbing right up to that wooden crossbeam towering over the place of the skull.

You could have sat in some silent celestial monastery and written volumes about Your love for me. You could have scripted it over the skies or pronounced it from the clouds—"I love you, Ruth. Come

share My Kingdom." Divine love could easily have
been passive love, and still I could have believed.

But divine love acted itself out. It was love
that made You take the nature of a servant, humble
Yourself, become obedient to death.[6] You worked
overtime for me. Gave up vacation rights. Canceled
Your pleasure. Shortened Your nights of sleep. You
rose before it was day, walked the midnight waves
on the Sea of Galilee because I was there in the boat,
frightened, doubting, in need of divine visitation.

You came when I needed You, on a wild and
windy night. Stretching out Your hand to me in my
failure, calming the chaos around me, reminding
me of a miracle. You could have sent Thomas to
identify with me in my doubt—if anyone knew
about doubt, he did. It had been a long day for
You, and the night air was bad for Your preaching
voice. But You braved the chill, pushed against the
north winds, steadied Yourself on water that rose
and fell in six-foot sheets, lifted me dripping wet
from my own humiliation, placed me firmly back
in the boat where I fell face-down and proclaimed,
"Truly you are the Son of God."[7]

How can I do less than answer one more call
for help coming through the night? How can I refuse
to ride the waves toward a group of bedraggled sail-
ors ready to fall overboard? How can I turn away
from one about to disappear beneath the waves?
Your love took You to the seas where people floun-
dered. My love for You must do the same. It is part
of the debt I owe.

It is also part of the feeling of indebtedness I
carry with me every waking and sleeping moment
(even in my sleep I work to make something hap-

pen). My debt is so vast it can never be paid—no matter what sacrifice, what activity, what doing and coming and going in the endless motions of love.

I work constantly to retire this debt. So my work is never done, for how does one know when her debt is paid? It is the debt of love I owe that seems to hover over me, like a heavy cloud threatening to descend. It doesn't go away. It changes shape and size as it moves across treetops, rooftops, telephone poles, but it's always there with its load of rain and pain and wearying effort.

I follow this cloud—or rather, it follows me. It is the obligatory side of love, which must work to show itself grateful. Work to show itself genuine. Work to show itself dedicated. Perhaps it must work just to *show* itself. How else will they know we are Christians if we don't live out our love?

Lord, I know this world needs more love. You are not here as a physical demonstration anymore, so we must pick up where You left off. "Show me love, don't tell me about love" is what they say when they are looking for reason not to believe. But it's the show that sometimes fatigues me. There is great pressure in being a showcase for divine love. The only portrait of Your love they may ever see is me. If they don't get the picture, surely I will be to blame. To have kept others from the Kingdom is serious business.

So my love must be conscientious; I must be careful not to mar the image. Your love is lofty; I must raise their sights. Your love is patient, kind. Does not envy or boast. Is not proud, rude, self-seeking, easily angered, keeps no record of wrongs. It does not delight in evil, but rejoices with truth, always protects, trusts, hopes, perseveres. *Never fails.*[8] As

I walk through the office door to pour myself a cup of coffee and chat over sweet rolls, I wonder, *Is it showing through yet, this divine love I should be exhibiting? What do they think of You now, dear Lord?*

Frankly, Father, I'm tired. Creating good press for You is intense work. Perhaps it's the political side of love that drains and wearies me. I feel I have to make You look good. I am out to influence souls for the Kingdom as though I am chalking one up on the side of love or gaining points for Your ratings. Public opinion counts. How are we doing this week? Down a point or two? If so, I have to double my effort.

I must confess here that my displays of love are not always so altruistic as they may seem. My deeds of devotion are sometimes for *my* welfare, not Yours. I am compelled to do love to make *me* look good. If I look good, if I love them, surely they will love me.

I want others to be impressed when they see my love in action. "My, how she loves. When does she ever find time to do it all?" I am motivated to whirlwind love because people seem to be impressed by movement. The more movement, the more proof that I am going someplace. The more action, the more love. People can see when I give up an afternoon to visit an invalid who hasn't left her apartment in five years. I have something to write about, something to share with others — all the blessings one receives from visiting invalids in solitary confinement. Perhaps my hearers or readers will be motivated to do likewise. And You know, dear Lord, how much invalids need visiting. Perhaps my example will challenge others to love not "with words or tongue but with actions and in truth."[9]

This is the exemplary side of love. But Lord, it is also an empty side of love. There is something hollow about visiting an invalid so that I have a story to tell. There is something mechanical about going through the motions without the heart, like playing drums without feeling the beat. I beat the drum. I produce. *Achieve. Accomplish. Create the whirlwind.* And by the time the dust settles, I have moved on to something else.

It's heavy, this mechanical love that grows from obligation. It is outwardly impressive, but inwardly oppressive—for *it must be done.* And when love *must* be done it is intense, tedious, pressured, and forever tired.

Yes, Lord. I am forever tired in my efforts to do love. It is a full-time job. Sometimes my hands do not move heartily in the service of Your love. In fact, today my hands hang limp. I do not feel like doing anything. I am spent, depleted, washed up on shore like an empty shell.

But my list is long! The Sunday school class needs teaching. The bathrooms need cleaning. The clothing needs ironing. An article is past deadline, and my neighbor is smarting from divorce.

But I do not feel like lifting a finger. The sun rises in the east, climbs higher in the sky, and seems to mock my inertia. The clock glares down at me from the mantel. Time to move. Time to go. Time to do. My list stares up at me from my desk, waiting for the check marks. Item accomplished. Sign of competence. Sign of productivity. Sign of love in action.

But this morning there are no signs. I do not move. I do not even want to move. Nothing inside has the will. The clock ticks on and my guilt grows. So much to do. So many to serve. So much harvest not yet in. "I have only just a minute, only sixty seconds in it. Forced upon me. Didn't seek it. Didn't choose it. But it's up to me to use it. I must suffer if I lose it. Give account if I abuse it. I have only just a minute, but eternity is in it." My childhood rhyme returns to haunt me.

If only I loved more deeply, I would be motivated to move. Goal for the day: to love more deeply. It is just one more thing I must add to my list of things to do. The sun grows hot. The Amalekites are winning the battle in the valley. I sit on the hilltop with Moses. I am losing. We are losing. My hands are tired. Aaron and Hur move in support. Even with the rock as my prop, I cannot hold up my hands. Aaron and Hur must hold them up for me.[10]

I cannot do it. I cannot do everything. Right now, I cannot do *anything*. I cannot do love.

I open my faded blue notebook that preserves notes from the years—clippings, quotes, Scriptures, stories. A poem is typed on unlined paper. It flutters to my lap.

What shall I do?
What shall I do?
Nothing.
Nothing is the thing to do.
Nothing is the only thing to do.
I am worthwhile just existing.
Just?
Okay. I am worthwhile existing.
What if the stars were to start doing something?
What are you doing, little hummingbird?

"I am just being a hummingbird."
Oh, is that all?
"As soon as I start doing,
I stop being."
I don't understand how you can do so little.
"Now that's a compliment."

I search in vain for the author, the source, some trace of origin. The words shock me. Never have I heard, "As soon as I start doing, I stop being." This is contrary to everything I have been taught. Everything I believe about loving in deed.

Now, through the empty ache of mechanical love, the tight shoulders and taut muscles from all the doing of love, the load of guilt for not doing more, comes Your voice, dear Lord, as surely as the clock ticks on the mantel. . . .

My child—come close. Put aside your list. I have built the fire. Come sit by Me.

Come rest in the secret place of the Most High, be at home in the shadow of the Almighty. Sing in the shelter of My wings. Cling to Me.[11] Oh how often I would gather you to Me, as a hen gathers her chicks under her wings, but you were not willing.[12] You were too busy doing, running hither and yon like a chicken with its head cut off.

I could not gather you while you were running. I could not close My arms of love around you while you were on your high-speed chase for the cause of My Kingdom. Neither could I tell you of My love. You cannot hear My love in whirlwinds;

I come in gentle whispers.[13] You must be close to hear gentle whispers. I carry the lambs in My arms, close to My heart.[14] Let Me carry you close.

Nothing brings Me more delight than to love you. But sometimes, child, you seem to have a hard time letting Me love you. It seems easier for you to scurry around doing love than to open yourself to letting Me love you. Do you want to know why? It's because doing love is good for your ego; sitting quietly and receiving love is humbling. Doing love puts you in charge; receiving love means I am the giver and you are the taker. (You find it safer to be the giver than the taker—less risky.) Doing love is high-profile; receiving love is what happens between you and Me in private. Doing love produces tangible results; receiving love has nothing to stack in the warehouse at the end of the day.

I am not surprised that you are wearied by the *doing* of love. When you think you can do all the loving, you *will* get weary. When you cannot receive, you *will* soon have nothing to give.

Let Me love you. I loved you before you did anything for Me, and if you never do another thing for Me, still I will love you. You accepted My love gift when, for the first time, you saw the cross. You believed then that I could love you enough to die for you. Why do you have such a hard time with the idea that My love for you did not stop at Calvary? My love for you today is just as strong as it was the day I hung by iron spikes and blood ran down My forehead for love of you.

I sent you My message of love on that day and in no uncertain terms you translated the telegram. But I want to tell you how much I love you *today.* I want to walk with you, talk with you, see you smile at the notes I send, watch your face light up when you hear Me say, "I will never leave you. I'm always here for you no matter what." Calvary was only the beginning—the wedding ceremony.

I want to give Myself to you in love every day. But I cannot if you are trying to do all the giving, all the loving. One-way love exhausts you and rejects Me.

I do not want your service; I want *you.* Remember Martha? She too thought the only way to love Me was to scurry around serving Me. The meal she prepared for Me was good. Her house was spotless. You are right—I like good food and clean houses. But not if they keep My loved ones from coming close and hearing My words of love for them. I wanted Martha more than I wanted the lunch she packed Me for the road. I wanted her to choose what Mary chose—to be with Me.[15] It is the greater side of love. It is the heart of love, the source from which all doing of love must spring. No river can flow without a source.

As for the work that needs to be done, there will *always* be work. You will always feel driven toward it. As a result of the curse, you will always feel the hardness of effort in it. You will always be tempted to substitute it for love, and you will often feel bound by it.

But work is not your payoff, your credit to be applied against the debits of your account. Your account is already settled.

The tendency to pay the debt in order to earn love has been around for centuries. You are right: you cannot pay your debt. You are too far in the hole. That is why I picked up the tab. And after I paid the bill, I sat down at My Father's right hand. It was finished. My work on your behalf was complete. You are out of the hole. You do not owe Me a thing.

So, then, enter My presence — not to pay the mortgage but to savor My love. Come to Me as though the slate is clear. *It is.* Come and enjoy My love. Leave your sense of indebtedness at the door.

As you come to Me released from the bondage of debt, hold your head high. Look Me in the eyes. Sit quietly, without lengthy explanations, without apologies, without promises to try harder or be more punctual with the payments. You do not have to hurry off to get back to work. You have nothing to pay. You are debt-free.

When it gets right down to it, My child, *you can do nothing for Me; I've done it all for you.* I do not need your service. My work will get done with or without you. I am before all things, and in Me all things hold together.[16] Everything held together before you came on the scene, and everything will hold together when you leave the scene. You need not work so hard at control.

I also know how hard you work to make Me look good, how conscientious your efforts before the watching world. True, they do watch. Your reproduction of Me is important. But I am not tarnished because what you do may blur My image sometimes.

Yours is not the only picture others have of Me. I paint Myself in the sunsets, write Myself on the ocean floor, print My footsteps in the clouds, plant My name among the redwoods. I imprint

43

Myself on people near and far. I am beyond your meager picture frame that houses My image. If you fail in your PR efforts, I am not without witness. Even the rocks cry out.

Don't worry about how I look because of you. It will only add another burden. The strain shows in your eyes, your forehead, your jaw. You will be a better picture of Me when you stop worrying about how you're doing on My behalf. Self-conscious love always mars the image because it focuses on you rather than on Me.

When you are full of being loved, you *will be* good press for Me. But you won't know it, because it will happen so naturally. There is a certain winsomeness about a person who is confident she is loved—a radiance others cannot overlook. It's part of the glory Moses wore on his face when he'd sat with Me awhile.[17] It is the sweet perfume of My Son.[18]

Come spend time with Me, and others will notice. "Here is one who is loved. She has nothing to prove. See how relaxed, how unpretentious. No tooting horn, waving banners, proclaimed accomplishments. She's comfortable to be around. Love is written all over her face." People who don't need to prove anything are My best representatives.

You want to know how to motivate others to do love? It isn't by doing more love so you can be their model. It's by coming close to Me, letting My love soak into you like water saturating a sponge. Others will know when you are full. When their lives touch yours, love will seep out. Then it will be My love that motivates them, not your deeds.

Choose one thing: to come near. As you do,

you will experience My love for you like you've never experienced it before. Everywhere you turn, you will discover My love—signed in your Bible, shining through the eyes of a friend, murmured gently among the fir trees along your morning walk.

You will wake to a new day with the thought, *I am loved.* You will move through the monotony, the disappointments, the weeds and thorns of your work, with the thought, *He loves me.* When you eat at midday you will remember, *I am His gift. This food is His gift.* And you will find strength for your afternoon. On your bed you will remember Me; you will think of Me throughout the night.[19] As you drift into sleep, you will know, *He's thinking of me.* And you will find rest for body and soul.

As you drink deeply of My love, you will be strengthened and renewed. Then the doing of your love will be the overflow. You will be so intoxicated with the thought, *I am loved,* that you will respond, "I love You too." Giving love will then be your expression of joy, like a bride on her wedding day. "I know you love me—therefore, I can say, 'in sickness and in health, in plenty and in want,' I will be there for you." When you learn how much I really love you, commitment will be no duty, only sheer delight. You will love because first you are loved.[20]

Receive My commitment to you. "I have loved you with an everlasting love; I have drawn you with loving-kindness."[21] Remember my gifts. Pull out the book of old love letters, reread them as you read them when love was new. Remember how much richer your life is because of My love. How I warmed you when you were cold. How I was there, searching for you in the crowd, when you were lonely. How I sat and waited for you when you forgot. How I smiled when you sang, cried when you hurt, listened when you needed to talk.

Remember our dreams for the future. Where did they go? Covered over by so much doing, so many lists and schedules, so many meetings that must be attended, so much motion and commotion, so much clutter and clamor and whirlwind dust.

And soon, as we sit together—remembering, receiving, renewing, laughing, crying, listening, talking—you will forget your lists. You will allow them to collect dust in the far corners of your bottom desk drawers. Your focus will be on Me and how much I love you rather than on you and how much you have to do.

Then the love will begin to trickle out. From deep within your well-watered heart, you will serve Me. But you will serve Me naturally, like an artesian well that cannot stop itself, so energized is its flow. No laborious pumping and priming, no schemes and diagrams and seminars on how to suck water out of the ground. It will come. Full force. Fresh. Thirst-quenching. Ever flowing because of its deep, hidden source.

Child, your doing of love must come from the abiding assurance that you are loved. You must *be* My love before you can *do* My love. Perhaps it is the greater side of faith for you to say, "I love You, Lord," and not do anything for me than it is to say, "I love You, Lord—here, let me take just one more project." If you love Me, yes, feed My lambs. But if you love Me, first *be* My lamb. And I carry My lambs close to My heart. . . .

The clock still ticks on the mantel. The bathrooms are still dirty, the deadline still unmet, the clothing still unironed, my neighbor still hurting.

I move to the backyard hammock, stretch out, and stare up into leafy green and background blue. No books. No radio. No lists. No menus. No phone. No pen. No paper. No index file. I feel no compulsion, no guilt, as the moments tick away. . . .

> *The sands of time are sinking,*
> *The dawn of heaven breaks.*
> *The summer morn I've sighed for,*
> *The fair, sweet morn awakes. . . .*
> *Oh, I am my Beloved's, and my Beloved's mine*
> *He brings a poor vile sinner*
> *Into his "house of wine. . . ."*
> *The Bride eyes not her garment,*
> *But her dear Bridegroom's face;*
> *I will not gaze at glory*
> *But on my King of grace.*
> *Not at the crown He giveth*
> *But on His pierced hand*
> *The Lamb is all the glory*
> *Of Immanuel's land.*[22]

> *I sit and gaze for a long, long time.*
> *What did I do today?*
> *Nothing.*
> *It's the most I've done in a long, long time. . . .*
> *Father,*
> *You have given me*
> *a place of peace*

47

close beside You,
near Your heart.
You have given me
a fortress of strength
a reservoir of love;
I feel it flow
from Your strong arms around me.
You are my calm:
I run to You when I am harried.
You are my restorer:
I come to You when I am empty.
You are my warm fire,
where I can safely
kick off my shoes
and rest awhile.

NOTES

1. 1 Timothy 5:8.
2. Luke 10:2, John 9:4.
3. Ecclesiastes 9:10.
4. Luke 12:48.
5. From the American folk hymn "What Wondrous Love Is This?" author unknown, 1835.
6. Philippians 2:5-8.
7. Matthew 14:22-33.
8. 1 Corinthians 13:4-8.
9. 1 John 3:18.
10. Exodus 17:8-13.
11. Psalm 63:7-8, 91:1
12. Matthew 23:37.
13. 1 Kings 19:11-13.
14. Isaiah 40:11.
15. Luke 10:38-42.
16. Colossians 1:17.
17. Exodus 34:29.
18. 2 Corinthians 2:14.
19. Psalm 63:6.
20. 1 John 4:19.
21. Jeremiah 31:3.
22. From the hymn "The Sands of Time Are Sinking" by Anne Ross Cousin (1824-1906).

3

I'M AFRAID OF LOSING LOVE
The Longing for Reassurance

omeone gave me a gift one day, when things were going well between us. But then times got tough, and she asked for her gift back.

I was eight years old and the gift was a fake silver friendship ring. I've grown up since then, and friends generally don't take back their friendship gifts. But still my world plays games with love. It uses love as reward or punishment. It withholds and withdraws affection, dangling it like a revocable gift on a string. "Do what I like and you can have my love. Disappoint me and you do without."

So You see, Lord, why I sometimes have trouble trusting love. I fear it might be taken back.

Love games hurt. Either I am reduced to a pawn or I become the wielder of power that doesn't rightfully belong to me. The one who moves the pawns is always in control. The one who is moved is always victim. We play out our relationships on a giant chessboard—in and out of check, here a winner, there a loser. Now you have it, now you don't. Life becomes very insecure, because with games, you're never sure of the bottom line. Am I playing for keeps? Will I come out the loser again?

Now, I admit—we can't live totally free of games. Parts of life inevitably turn up win or lose. I have participated in innocent sports and survived. I have lost reward when someone scored higher than I and claimed the prize. I have lost an election or two, a committee seat, a bid for first or second or third place. Sometimes I win, sometimes I don't; but nothing ventured, nothing gained.

Losing at games or elections or ratings is one

thing: We learn from it and go on. But losing the love of another is something else: It is a nightmare. To suffer the displeasure of one we love is bad enough. To be deserted by love is quite possibly the worst torture of the soul.

I live in a world that not only plays games with love, it pollutes love with threats, betrayals, and desertions. I stand in line at the grocery store and scan the tabloids before me—broken love, in one form or another, screams from every cover. Commitments that didn't count. Cheap promises gone down the drain with the first wash of innocence. I do not turn the pages on such drama, but I leave the check-out counter with the sinking reminder that to form attachments is to risk loss. To love is to lose.

Even the kind of love that lifts itself high above soap opera melodrama and cheap headlines carries with it the risk of loss. No matter how faithfully proclaimed the vow, there is always the unknown, the unforeseen, the unpredictable lurking around the corner, waiting to snatch away what we count on most.

Love falls victim to change, and change is everywhere. No wonder I feel love must, after all, at some time, for some reason, change. People change their minds—and sometimes, minds change people. An Alzheimer's victim, roams the halls of her nursing home without a trace of recognition for the one she's loved and lived with faithfully for fifty years. My good friend, giver of love and delight, packs a moving van and moves to another part of the country.

This is the way of all creation—now you see

it, now you don't. Life changes. Love changes. Love loses. I lose.

And dear Lord, *I don't like the thought of losing love.* I want arms of affection around me forever. I want favor. I want reassurance.

One of the hardest of all crosses for me is the thought that someone is displeased with something I've said or done—be it simply a ticket for overextending my welcome in a municipal parking lot; a note from a friend reminding me I haven't written for two months; a frown on the librarian's face when I tell her I can't find the book I borrowed three weeks ago; or what sounds to me like a long, bothered sigh from my husband when I forget to leave the keys in their usual place.

Why such a big deal—the sigh, the frown, the overdue letter, the five-dollar parking ticket? Everyone forgets now and then. Everyone misjudges from time to time, does something thoughtless. Everyone's depravity shows in some way or other. I am bound to displease someone, no matter how hard I try to do otherwise. Why not simply acknowledge imperfection and forget the responses to my misdemeanors? Why bother about whether they are smiling or frowning at me?

Perhaps it has to do with my strong desire to please. I want to know that I bring pleasure to others—to see their smile of approval, their look of delight over some word, action, or deed of mine. I don't like storms—not in the skies, not on the face of someone looking at me. I run from wrath, cringe at harsh judgments, crawl far back into my shell of silence when I feel displeasure is brewing. *They're unhappy with me. They think badly of me. I let them down — disappoint them, inconvenience them, frustrate them, anger them.* I do not want to stay around to face the consequences.

Yes, that's it: I fear the consequences. I fear judgment. Punishment. Sentences. Penalties. Pronouncements. Misunderstanding. I fear withdrawal — the agony of being ignored — that silent, invisible barrier that makes someone look at me without seeing me, transfer allegiance to one more favored, depart in spirit, as if to a far country. The longest distance is between two hearts.

When favor goes, love disappears. Such is the way of human love. Lord, I know it is not Your way. I am Your child. I can tick off Your attributes: You do not leave me when I've hurt You, go into Your silent shell when I've ignored You, transfer Your faithfulness to someone else when I've been untrue. But I must confess, sometimes I see Your love through fickle, human eyes. I pluck the daisy petals: *He loves me; He loves me not.* I reach cautiously for Your love because there are holes in my heart — holes carved out by lost favor, lost love, lost affection, lost presence. Here today. Gone tomorrow.

I know better about Your love. You are made up of love. It runs in Your veins. You cannot help but love, even as a star cannot help but shine. I've read about Your immutability — Your unchanging nature. I've studied it. Written papers for theology class about it. Taught it. Spoken it. Sung it:

> O the deep, deep love of Jesus, vast, unmeasured, boundless, free! Rolling as a mighty ocean in its fullness over me, underneath me, all around me, is the current of Thy

love; leading onward, leading homeward
to my glorious rest above. O the deep,
deep love of Jesus, spread His praise from
shore to shore! How He loveth, ever loveth,
changeth never, nevermore; how He watches
over His loved ones, died to call them all His
own; how for them He intercedeth, watcheth
over them from the throne.[1]

But sometimes, Lord, I still fear losing Your
favor. I clutch after reassurance of Your approval,
press through the crowd to lay hold of it like the
woman suffering from a blood disease who touched
the hem of Your garment in her desperate need for
healing.[2]

I am like that woman, reaching out to make
sure You are here for me.

"Who touched My clothes?"

I tremble in the indictment and stand shiver-
ing as I await my sentence. I should not have touched
You. Women neither touched nor were touched by
men of the cloth. In fact, religious leaders went to
great lengths to avoid even so much as a glance
toward a woman.

Besides—I am unclean, contaminated by disease. The Law is harsh in its penalty for contact with
the unclean. I defile You by my touch. I am guilty of
violating religious taboos.

I should not have touched You. But I did. I
need to touch You.

Sometimes I hear Your voice—gentle, warm,
full of love and understanding: "Daughter, your
faith has healed you. Go in peace and be freed from
your suffering." It is Your voice of acceptance as it

was to her then, those two thousand years ago in the peaceful Galilean lake district.

But that voice is not the one I hear today, driving alone through rush-hour traffic, headed home from the city: "Ruth! Why did you say that? You left yourself open to all kinds of misunderstanding. You should have been more careful with your facts and details. Misrepresentation is serious business."

I hear a voice of judgment. I hear displeasure. Penalty. As if a judge were pronouncing sentence, I hear the pound of the gavel: "The mouths of liars will be silenced."[3] I shiver in the cold. "Oh, Lord, was it lying, this carelessness with the truth, this embellishing of details? I am a storyteller—so was my grandfather and my father. Telling good stories runs in my genes; it's part of the process of good communication to illustrate. How do You silence Your children? Does it hurt very much? Take very long?" I cower in the distance I feel from You.

I feel distance, yes, and I feel Your displeasure. I am orphaned to the snow, even now as it splatters against my windshield. It comes so fast my wipers can't keep up with it. *Guilty. Guilty. Guilty.* You have stated clearly how You despise misrepresentation of the truth. "There are six things the LORD hates, seven that are detestable to him: haughty eyes, a lying tongue. . . ."[4]

I am consumed with my misrepresentation. I vow to do better next time, to be more exact, more precise. Please, Lord, I beg for Your mercy to forgive a careless tongue.

But I cannot forget. My image of Your displeasure pursues me into a fretful sleep. I see Your eyes narrowed to a slit. Jaw set. Lips straight and unsmiling. No delight in those who misrepresent. You are holding court, and You are the judge. I stand guilty before Your throne. Shoulders stooped. Eyes downcast. Hands clasped tightly before me. I have lost Your approval. I feel the pain of alienation.

Tonight I feel a long way from home. I am a prodigal child.[5] But I have been prodigal before, over other issues, bigger issues than this. I remember them all now as I wade through the mud. The distance from home increases.

I am in a pigpen. Yes, in a pigpen feeding pigs. I was not meant for pigpens. I am a daughter, but I am not worthy. I did not mean to come here. I do not want to be here.

It was so much better in Your house, dear Father. But I was careless. Squandered my inheritance. Just a minor misrepresentation, not deliberate lying. No big deal. But still I am feeding pigs—a consequence of my own guilt. I am no longer wearing robes of celebration, the ring of daughtership, shoes that mean I'm home. I am in a distant land. I have displeased.

I am worried, Lord. When one chooses pigpens—no matter how momentary the stay—why should You hang around? I have created distance. Sin separates, causes You to turn Your back. You would not follow me to the pigpen of my choosing. Surely You would not dirty Your feet in the mud with me. Pigpens do not become Your dignity.

Neither do ash heaps. I sit with Job on his ash heap and wonder where I might find You. Was it the consequence of my sin that drove You away? My comforters say so. I cannot find You, no matter where I look. If I go to the east, You are not there; if

I go to the west, I do not find You. When You are at work in the north, I do not see You; when You turn to the south, I catch no glimpse of You.[6] Surely, my sins have hid You from me.[7]

I do deserve Your absence: "Those who plow evil and those who sow trouble reap it."[8] Job's friends were right. Misrepresent the facts and when you show up for dinner, no one will be there for the pleasure of your company. Express your anger over ash heaps and God will move on—maybe to others who can give their testimony of praise in public with a clear conscience.

Maybe You will bestow the blessing on them instead of me. They are full of praise while I fall short of truth. Surely they have endeared themselves to You because of their deep spirituality while I grow cold on the ash heap. Perhaps You will transfer the birthright to some other favorite child. I don't want to be stuck eating porridge for the rest of my life while the blessing that could have been mine substitutes another in the royal lineup.[9]

Without Your favor, Lord, there is no blessing. What is life like without Your blessing? I tremble at the thought. "Miss the will of God and you will live without the smile of God." Such admonition sticks fast in memories from the past. I am Your child, yes. But what if I miss Your plan for me? What if I lose Your favor? What if I forfeit the blessing? One wrong move and the ax could fall. I tiptoe gingerly, fearful lest I waken prematurely the wrath that is to come.

On that great and terrible day of wrath, I will stand before You while the books are opened. I will be judged according to what I have done as it is recorded in Your book.[10] The tape recorder is playing. Notes are being taken. Actions observed. Attitudes checked. You are keeping score. You are the judge, the referee who metes out the penalties.

I stand to lose my reward. Does it hurt very much to lose a reward? Would You smile as You place a three-star crown on my head even if You knew I could be wearing five stars? Will some of the tears You wipe from my eyes be tears I shed because I've let You down? The thought of being a disappointment to my Father is a hard thought for me:

> By and by when I look on His face. Beautiful face. Tear stained face. By and by when I look on His face. I'll wish I had given Him more. More so much more. More of my life than I'd ever given before. By and by when I look on His face, I'll wish I had given Him more.[11]

My record is not as good as it might have been, not as good as You'd hoped it would be. Will I feel Your displeasure even as I stand before You? I see the courtroom scene as clearly as I pictured the Swiss Alps years before I got there. I anticipated the Swiss Alps. But, Lord, this picturing of judgment is not an anticipation.

Will You hand out stiff sentences to Your children for failure to meet their quota? Do You hand out stiff sentences today for stretching the truth? For bypassing Your plan? Do You exile delinquents to the backside of the desert until they've learned their lesson and can return to usefulness? I fear the shelf, Lord. I fear removal of the power. I fear being disbarred. One wrong step and I'm banished to the desert.

I know the story well. I am like Moses. I have displeased You. Taken matters into my own hands. Imagined I could do the liberating myself. Knocked off an Egyptian. Hid my sin in the dirt and doomed myself to nonusefulness for a significant chunk of my life.

Now Your power has gone; I am reduced to tending sheep. Your presence is gone; I no longer see You in the marbled halls of Pharaoh's palace, no longer hear Your voice through those of the royal household who care for me. I live alone on the desert shelf, removed from divine appointment. (Nothing could have been more divinely appointed than a tiny basket containing a Hebrew baby boy, sailing smoothly into the hands of an Egyptian princess.) I am alone in the desert because of sin and disfavor. All because I have let You down, violated one of the ten commandments before it was even given.

I am sitting on a desert shelf of sorts, misrepresentations forgotten, but still worried over the myriad sins that so easily entangle. The woods grow thick outside the window of this quiet retreat center, and the robins have started their spring search for worms in the newly thawed ground. Tiny green shoots are on the verge of eruption, but I am so absorbed in shortcomings that I barely take notice.

I wonder, Lord, about Your power, Your presence, Your blessing, Your smile of approval. The traces seem so faint these days. I have not felt any great surges of power, seen any "miracles of blessing" recently. No letters of commendation. No first-person testimonials on how You've worked through me. No swinging wide of opportunity's doors. No significant requests for my services. I do not even know if You are still working through me. Have I done something wrong?

This center is a place of silence. Through my open window the woods are quiet. The robins chirp but I do not know their language. Even the sisters I sit beside at the noon meal say nothing. Garbed in muted black and white and gray, they simply smile as they pass the salt and pepper and pat me on the arm as I rise to go. "Day of personal spiritual retreat" were the only words I had written on the form when I checked in earlier this morning. It is a day of quiet.

But today I am disquieted by quiet. Today I feel the silence is Your sentence upon me—as if I have been banished to the desert for my impetuousness. I am caught up with confession. Preoccupied with the thought of Your displeasure. Absorbed in my "I wish I had given Him more" lament. I have spent the morning looking inward.

> What a wretched [woman] I am! . . . I am unspiritual, sold as a slave to sin. I do not understand what I do. For what I want to do I do not do, but what I hate I do. And if I do what I do not want to do . . . it is no longer I myself who do it, but it is sin living in me. I know that nothing good lives in me, that is, in my sinful nature. For I have the desire to do what is good, but I cannot carry it out. For what I do is not the good I want to do; no, the evil I do not want to do—this I keep on doing. Now if I do what I do not want to do, it is no longer I who do it, but it is sin living in me that does it.[12]

Judgment. Condemnation. I am back in the courtroom again, waiting out the consequence. Have You withdrawn Your favor, Lord? I do not feel we are as close today as we were six months ago. Have You moved on, closer to someone who has more time for You? Am I still useful to You? My phone does not seem to be ringing as often as it used to.

Do I still have Your blessing? It's lonely to think I may have lost closeness with You because I have displeased You or not lived up to Your perfect will for my life (whatever that is). Perhaps I've settled for second best and now You are walking behind me instead of beside me. Perhaps I have built my golden calf and now we are mere acquaintances rather than face-to-face, up-close friends like You and Moses.[13]

Lord, *I need to know.* Do Your eyes still smile when You look on me? Would You cancel an appointment just to come home and be with me? Do You walk with me in the rain showers just because I enjoy doing it? Am I still Your pleasure, even in my half-hearted, lukewarm, bungling attempts at love?

It's time for five o'clock vespers. I slip into my shoes, close the door to my room, and walk the soft carpets toward the chapel. The chimes have already begun, and the red and gold tapestries above the altar reflect the late afternoon sun.

I see the tapestries, yes—but even more, I see Your hand, scripting letters among the sun's rays. I read Your message as certainly as if Western Union had delivered it straight from the throne room. I slip into a pew and stare upward, above the altar. You are there waiting for me. Waiting to reassure. I am brought from my introspection to You. Perhaps it is where You have wanted me all along.

> You know me . . . you have laid your hand upon me. . . . Where can I go from your Spirit? Where can I flee from your presence? If I go up to the heavens, you are there; if I make my bed in the depths, you are there. If I rise on the wings of the dawn, if I settle on the far side of the sea, even there your hand will guide me, your right hand will hold me fast. . . . You created my inmost being; you knit me together in my mother's womb. . . . I am fearfully and wonderfully made; your works are wonderful, I know that full well.[14]

Lord, here in this place of silence, sitting on the desert shelf of my own making, I hear Your words of love. . . .

I am here for you, child. I have always been here for you; I will always be here for you.

You are My pleasure. Feel My arm around you? My hand in yours? I have not withdrawn My embrace. I hold you tightly. I go where you go. In fact, you cannot go anywhere that I am not—pigpens, ash heaps, desert shelves. I walk beside you—not before, not behind, but next to you, like good friends do. I hang on to you.

You are My creation, and you are wonderful. Would I desert My own creation because of her lapses? Would I leave My handiwork to mourn on

ash heaps alone? To brace against the desert winds without My presence? To wallow through muddy pigpens on her own?

You are My delight, whether you are good, bad, or indifferent. True, I do not always delight in what you do, but I always delight in you. My love for you is unfailing.[15] Unfailing love goes beyond pigpens, ash heaps, and exaggerations. You're right, such places are not of My choosing for you. They do not become My holiness, nor the holiness I desire for you. But you are My pleasure. You have always been My pleasure. You will always *be* My pleasure. You *are* My pleasure whether you *do* My pleasure or not. This is what makes My love different from yours.

I know that sometimes you will settle for husks in a pigpen when you could be having steak at My table. It is the way of all humanness. Unfailing love waits patiently — sits there on the fence by the pigpen and watches the sorry sight, pained that you should have to slop through the mud for a while.

Yes, I'll wait for you to get your fill of tending pigs. From the house I'll be looking out the windows, down the road, fifteen times a day. Wondering if today might be the day. Wiping tears because of the wall between us, the wall erected by your indifference to Me — not by My indifference to you.

Unfailing love does not grow cold waiting for your return. My lamps are always burning for you. The robes are always ready. The ring is polished, shoes ready by the back door. You are My loved one. Bone of My bone. Flesh of My flesh.

I knit you together while you were still in your mother's womb—would I forget you when you come unraveled?

I am here for you when you push through the crowd, violate the social taboos to touch My garment. I am here for you when you have eaten so many corn husks you lose appetite for My food; when you have tended sheep for so many years you forget what it's like to serve My people; when you sit on your ash heap and wish to die.

I was there for you before the morning stars sang together. I am here for you when the snowstorm assaults you on the freeway. And I will be there for you when you stand before the open book. I will be there beside you when I show you what might have been. I will help you through that pain. But I will also welcome you home with "Well done, good and faithful servant! . . . Come and share your master's happiness!"[16]

Unfailing love does not go away, even though the loved one may. Unfailing love follows close behind. "Never will I leave you; never will I forsake you."[17] Remember, I am not the one who turns My back. I turned My back once. It was enough. It took care of disfavor forever. Now we can enjoy the pleasure of each other's company—depending on what you decide.

Do not fear losing My love. *Do not fear Me.* Come to Me as a child to her father. Respect Me for My position as your Father, but do not cower from Me.

There is a difference between fear and respect. Fear drives people apart; respect brings them together. When you respect your father, you look for ways to make him happy. When you fear him, you hide or look for ways to avoid getting caught. When you respect your father, you can open your heart to him. When you fear him, you close up your heart and lock him out. You may serve and obey him, but you will not enjoy him. Respect frees you to focus on him; fear consumes you with threatening consequences.

Yes, there will be consequences to your choices. You and I must both deal with them. You will forget Me from time to time. I cannot help but feel your forgetfulness; you cannot help but suffer from your forgetfulness. I mourn the consequences, grieve over the pain you create for yourself, long for your healing and our restoration. But I do not drag you to the bench and pound My gavel: "Order in the court." I do not stand over you with flashing eyes and fiery words: "Why did you do that . . . ? How could you . . . ? Didn't you remember . . . ? You should have known better!"

Courtrooms are fearful places. I can see why you fear Me if you think I'm always holding court on you. "Fear has to do with punishment. The one who fears is not made perfect in love."[18] My delight is not to judge you, My child (though sometimes I must remind you of the standard); My delight is to love you.

Now I know that you will not always be comfortable having Me around. Standards are never very comfortable. I represent all you could be but aren't, all you've done that you wish you hadn't. Wrong always squirms in the presence of the one wronged.

Because I am love, I will remind you of all

you are not when your teenager misses curfew and keeps you up and worried until all hours of the morning. Because I am patient, I will remind you of your impatience when you fuss over someone's lateness. Because I am faithful, I will remind you of your disloyalties. Because I am truth, you will not be able to look Me in the eye when you have been careless with it.

I am your standard. Standards, as safe as they are for you, will always feel a bit like sandpaper against your skin. They will make you feel guilty because they hold you accountable. But there is no other way you can know what is expected of you. I am your standard: not for your irritation, but for your safety. Imagine the chaos if there were no fences, if all the world were public beach. My standards for you are not a punishment but a proof of My love. I love you so much I want to protect you. Accept My laws as My arms of love around you, not as My finger pointing at you.

So you must understand, dear one, that I do not set standards in order to dangle a friendship ring, not to punish or reward your response. I set standards for you because they are good for you. If you break them I am sorry for you, but I do not withdraw My love, My presence, My power, or My blessing from you. Sometimes broken standards mean you cannot feel My presence, you cannot sense My power or My blessing—but this is not because I would not give them to you. It is because you have chosen not to receive them for a while. Something else has filled your affections. I cannot claim affections when they are already full. And I am not one to force Myself on another.

Don't fear loss of My favor. Don't fear that I will declare you disqualified and set you on the desert shelf. Your usefulness to Me is not based on your fitness; I use raw clay to fashion My pots. I delight in using the weak things to confound the mighty.[19] True, you may disqualify yourself by your own carelessness, laziness, or lack of repentance. Shelves of inaction are your own making, never Mine. But even when you put yourself on the shelf, I am there with you.

My child, "Fear not, for I have redeemed you; I have summoned you by name; you are mine. . . . I will be with you. . . . For I am the LORD, your God."[20]

I will be with you always, even when it appears I have withdrawn My presence. You must know, you must believe with all your heart, that I will never withhold My love from you as punishment for your omissions and commissions. When it seems that I have withdrawn the blessing — when nothing in your life seems to be working — you must know you are not sitting in the penalty box. You are simply experiencing the ebb and flow of your tired, old, fallen world — the ebb and flow of your tired, old, fallen self.

You must know I still walk the road to Emmaus with you.[21] You are lonely. Discouraged. Disappointed. Doubting. Feeling that perhaps you have let Me down. You think, had you stood your ground, perhaps I would never have faced the Roman executioners. I have gone, it seems — banished from the earth by the whims of politicians, religious leaders, the fickle crowd, and cowardly friends. If only all of you who claimed to love Me had not fallen asleep in the garden, you think. If only you had not cowered in fear around a late-night fire. If only you had appealed to the supreme court, sent out petitions, stood your ground. You would still have your friend and leader.

But you did desert Me, left Me to anguish alone. I have reason to take off for the celestial courts without saying goodbye. I have reason to teach you a lesson on loyalty you will not soon forget. Tell Me—should I disappear through the clouds without getting back in touch, so you know what it feels like to be deserted? After all, I am responsible for your learning.

But unfailing love sticks around even when loved ones fall asleep in the crisis hour. I keep coming back because I love you. I walk the road to Emmaus with you because I want to be with you this one last time. You are tired. I see dark circles under your eyes. I made your eyes, and I love them, even though they can't stay awake through My anguish, even though they can't see Me when I'm walking right beside you.

No wonder you can't see Me. You are absorbed in your own grief and failure. And now, on this dusty road, you are tired and hungry. I know about your hunger. When we get to Emmaus, I sit down at your dinner table, pick up a knife and slice the bread for your strawberry jam.

I know that there is nothing more lonely than slicing your own bread and eating strawberry jam alone, especially if you have the sinking feeling in the pit of your stomach that someone you loved dearly has gone, and it would be because you didn't do enough for him.

Here, let Me slice your bread for you. Let Me sit opposite the table from you and look lovingly into your tired and drooping eyes. Let Me tell you one more time how much I love you. How much I missed you when I had to turn My back on you awhile to cover your shortcomings once and for all so that from here on, I can be your Savior and not your judge. I left you once because of your sin. I will never leave you again. I am here at your dinner table as proof.

And even tomorrow, when the clouds come to take Me away, I will not have gone from you. You will hear Me say before I ascend, "I'm with you always. I'm with you always, even to the very end."[22] Sin will never again have power to separate us from each other.

So how could ash heaps and pigpens and misrepresentation of the truth and a splintered cross ever keep Me from you? They may keep you from Me, but they will never keep Me from you. Even a Roman execution could not keep Me from coming to you again.

I followed you to Emmaus, yes, and today I follow you wherever you go. I keep showing up, wherever you are, walking the roads you walk, sitting in the seat beside you as you drive, hovering close to you in a silent retreat center as you worry about courtroom scenes.

I do not go away. You must believe it. Believe it with all your heart: "He will never leave me." Say it to yourself when you awake to each new morning. Repeat it slowly throughout the day. Drift into sleep with the words on your lips.

And then, when you are as certain of My love and faithfulness as you are that the sun will rise tomorrow in the east, *you will be free to let Me love you.* You will rush to the door when I come home because My presence will bring you joy, not dread. You will relax, even in your fallings-short, because you know I will not walk away in retaliation. You will not need to fear others. You will be able to have joy in their successes rather than worry that I have switched My blessing to them.

You will not be afraid to blaze a trail through the forest—the one you never dared before, lest it turn out to be the wrong path and you wind up walking alone. When you are certain that I will not fly home if the trip with you gets too irritating, when you know I will go on with you no matter what, you will be confident. You will act like the daughter of royalty that you are because you know the adoption papers have been finalized. No one or nothing can snatch you away.[23] I will not give you up, nor will I leave you. You belong to Me. I belong to you.

In the reassurance of My approval and love, your eyes will be bright with belonging, your hands will relax in Mine. You will move with grace in a deliberate, purposeful stride.

Now you can be certain about Me. The guessing games are over. You are no longer the beggar, pleading for My blessing, My presence, My love. You have Me—My love, My pleasure, My presence, My blessing. You need not even ask. You are secure. You have nothing to lose. *I'm with you always.*

The vespers end. The sun has dropped lower in the west. The gilded edges of the tapestries are darker now.

"Go in peace. Grow in grace." The benediction falls like some heavenly amen. I am Jacob, receiver of the blessing. I am Jacob, sometimes deceiver, sometimes wrestler with God, sometimes alien in a strange land. But I am also Jacob, beloved child. I hear the words of blessing even as I move toward the evening shadows of the day. "Jacob will again have peace and security, and no one will make him afraid."[24]

My Father looks down the lane and sees me coming. He runs to meet me, garments flying. His love knows no limits. My robe is ready. He slips the ring on my finger, shoes on my tired, dusty feet. Then He draws me close. I feel His heartbeat and I know I am home. "There is no fear in love. But perfect love drives out fear."[25]

As I drive home from this quiet place, toward dinner and my family, I never once wonder whether I've pleased You today, Lord. I do think of You, sitting there at the other side of the table, slicing bread for my strawberry jam.

> *I am late.*
> *I have kept You waiting,*
> *taken up Your time.*
> *For a while*
> *something else was more important.*
> *I am distracted*
> *distant*

worried about consequences.
I come to You
mind full of excuses
hands shaking from the rush
ashamed for my lateness
fearful You might have gone on.

But You are there —
patiently waiting
sipping Your coffee.
Waiting
as though You have all the time in the world
    for me.

You take my trembling hand in Yours:
"Relax. I'm not going anywhere."
I take a deep breath.
I am calmed.
I am reassured.
I am loved.

NOTES
 1. From the hymn "O the Deep, Deep Love of Jesus" by Samuel
    Trevor Francis (1834-1925) and Thomas J. Williams, 1890.
 2. Mark 5:25-34.
 3. Psalm 63:11.
 4. Proverbs 6:16-17.
 5. Luke 15:11-32.
 6. Job 23:8-9.
 7. Isaiah 59:2.
 8. Job 4:8.
 9. Genesis 27:1-40.
10. Revelation 20:11-12.
11. Author unknown.
12. Romans 7:24,14-20.
13. Exodus 33:11, Deuteronomy 34:10.
14. Psalm 139:1,5,7-10,13-14.
15. Psalm 107.

16. Matthew 25:21.
17. Hebrews 13:5.
18. 1 John 4:18.
19. 1 Corinthians 1:27-29.
20. Isaiah 43:1-3.
21. Luke 24:13-35.
22. See Matthew 28:20.
23. John 10:27-29.
24. Jeremiah 30:10.
25. 1 John 4:18.

4

BUT I DON'T REALLY KNOW
FOR SURE
The Longing for Evidence

oday it is spring. I see the evidence. Tiny crocuses push up through winter remnants. The sun shines. Temperatures soar. Robins sing. It is not hard to believe in spring.

But last week was a different story. The calendar said spring but the sullen, steel-gray skies were spitting white pellets that stung my skin and rattled against the car. I slushed through the cold gray days like a robot wound up for movement but lacking heart. I did not see spring. I did not feel spring. I did not think spring.

For all practical purposes, last week I did not even believe in spring. I certainly did not live as if it were here. I didn't fill the birdbath with water, because there were no robins. I didn't open up my house, because there weren't any spring breezes. I made no movement toward the storage closet, for I had no need of spring clothes. No urges to head for the garden center to buy spring conditioners and plantings. Spring? Hardly.

I find it difficult to believe in spring, Lord, when I see no signs. And sometimes I find it hard to believe You love me like You say You do when I see no evidence—when the ground is still frozen, and the skies are stormy, and life seems to ask of me more than I have to give, and I sit lonely in my room awaiting Your answers.

You see, I am a person who needs evidence in order to believe in love. I need to see love standing at the door when I come home, waiting to welcome me with open arms. I need to see eyes looking at me in tenderness, brimming with joy at my presence, with tears at my pain. I need to see a hand reaching over the table for mine in comfortable companionship.

I need love to ride along with me in the car when I have to run an unexpected errand, need to hear simple statements of observation—"Look how fast the clouds are moving," or "Can you believe, another high-rise!" or "Doesn't it feel good just to get out"—signs that it takes no great amount of entertainment for love to enjoy being together.

I need to hear the words *I love you*. I need to see a presence. Touch the evidence. I need love sitting in the flesh beside me.

Dear Lord, is it such a great offense to need evidence of love? After all, You created me. Maybe some of Your creation can live comfortably without palpable reinforcements of love. But I need a love I can touch. Why? I don't know—maybe because I bonded well with my mother in my early years. Maybe I imprinted the memory of her skin next to mine, the hours she held me close and rocked me, her soft voice always answering "Here I am" when I called "Mommy!"

Perhaps I need love in the flesh because of my southern roots: everyone hugged everyone. Touch showed how you felt toward another. It reinforced how another felt toward you. How else did you know you were welcomed, loved, and free to come back for another visit? "Ya'll hurry back" was always accompanied by a hearty embrace. It made me feel that my hostess really liked having me around. I grew up with love signs posted every ten feet. No wonder evidence of love is important to me today.

Perhaps it's the romantic in me that visualizes love—what it looks like, where it goes, what it says, how it acts. It is not hard for me to give love a name, a face, a setting. "They are in love. Can't you tell by the way he looks at her and reaches for her hand?" "He loves me. I can see by the note he left on my pillow." I look for signs of love, as eagerly as a robin searches the grass for the first worm of spring. Signs are confirming. Signs are comforting.

And then too, Lord, I am part of a generation that looks for signs (much like the generation of Your time on earth). Some of my generation watch the skies and the newspapers for signs that some vague impersonal force is with them. While most of us who are Your children would not think of drawing daily guidance from signs in the sky or charts in the newspaper, sometimes we clutch as eagerly for evidence of love based on the size of our bank accounts, the condition of our health, the growth of our ministries, the professions that our children choose. Such signs must surely mean You love us.

I must admit, I do feel better when I see signs that You are working in the lives of my children — that this year they are reading the Bible more often than they did last year. I am more confident that You love me when I see enough money coming in to pay the bills each month, when the basement does not leak every time it rains, when the doctor's report is good. It's not hard to be convinced of Your love when all the vital signs are stable.

I am of my generation. But I am of Your generation too. I sit on a grassy knoll in the remote plains of the Decapolis.[1] I have come to hear You teach, yes, but I am also here to see the signs. Signs are important for belief. Otherwise, how will I know for sure?

You don't disappoint me. It's been three days

since my last meal. My stomach is empty. The bread-baskets are empty, and it's a long way to the nearest bakery. Now would be a good time to receive a sign, Lord. I need bread. I shoot a one-minute prayer arrow straight to Heaven: "Help needed. Lord, send the bread like You did for Moses and the people of Israel. Manna from Heaven. Good for the body. Good for the soul. Good for my faith."

You send the love sign, stroll through the crowd producing bread as though You'd been elbow deep in yeast since two this morning. I fill my plate. Stuff my pockets. Take some extra just in case. There's plenty for all. Your love is lavish.

I feel hugged by Heaven. Reaffirmed by the sign. Renewed in confidence that You do love me and remember me when I am sitting far from the bakery, without any bread. "What a God of love!" I write in my journal. It will be a good illustration for my next article. I am comfortably satisfied and strong in faith.

But You sigh as we get into the boat and follow You to the next region. Your sigh is deep and long. You look past the rolls that bulge in my pockets (one never knows when the bread supply may run low again), past my strong and well-fed body. You look to my heart. You disrupt my preoccupation with love signs. Why is it so important that You came to me there on the grassy plains and showed me love by filling my breadbasket? "Why does this generation ask for a miraculous sign?"[2] You come straight to the point, but I cannot answer Your question.

I don't know why we ask for a sign. Maybe because we are hungry. Maybe because we think only of ourselves. Maybe because we are insecure.

Maybe because we don't trust each other anymore and have to get it all in writing first. Maybe because we are accustomed to miracles, to tangible evidence, to frequent strokes of affirmation. Maybe we ask for a sign because we live in a show-and-tell world; *visual* is the word for our day. If we don't see love in real life, we can see it on the screen. Either way, our appetite is whetted but somehow never satisfied. For it seems that the more we see signs of love, the more signs of love we want to see.

"Why does this generation ask for a miraculous sign?" I am silenced by Your question, dear Lord. I hear weariness in Your sigh, as though You don't quite know what to do with us. I sit on the shore and wait for You to speak. Finally You break the silence. You have decided. "I tell you the truth," Your words cut deep; Your eyes are misty, "no sign will be given to [this generation]."[3]

But You just gave us a sign. Posting signs of love for Your children does not violate Your nature. You are love, and You are divine—capable of creating sun, moon, stars, and baskets full of bread. Besides, signs are proof of Your deity—evidence desperately needed if an unbelieving world is to be convinced.

Then, too, there is Your love for Your children—love so great it sometimes spills right out of Your soul and shows up in miracles. You care about empty stomachs. I could see Your look of tenderness even as You passed out the rolls. No more signs? No more breadbaskets filled to overflowing? Why the miracles at all if we aren't supposed to ask for more?

You have said what needs to be said. I watch as You get back into the boat and cross to the other side of the lake. I am left with a sinking feeling as I watch Your small craft disappear. No more signs. I listen to the waves lap against the shore.

Is love really love if there are no signs of it? How does my faith grow if I don't see the extraordinary in my life from time to time? Will others want Your love if they don't see some miracle in my life that would make them desire You? What do I have to pass on to others if I can't say, "See how great He is. See what He can do. He is a God worth trusting because He fills empty hearts, empty stomachs, empty pocketbooks. If He sent a daily dose of heavenly manna to Moses, He can do the same for you"?

I need evidence. Anyone can produce cheap words of love, sweep me off my feet with bold declarations. What touches my heart is proof. "Jesus loves me, this I know. For the Bible *tells* me so. . . ." I am awed by the words—but frankly, sometimes telling is just not enough.

I walk to the outskirts of the camp, where the rocks hang precariously from mountain cliffs. Like Moses, I have journeyed with You all these many years and never once seen Your face. Do You know how hard it is to walk with a person and see traces of a presence but never a face? I want to see You close up. I'm tired of veiled love.

Please don't get me wrong. I'm grateful for the traces You've left. You have signaled love to me, loud and clear. But Lord, I'm human. I want to look into Your eyes, reach out and touch Your face. I echo Moses' plea: "Now show me your glory."[4]

Glimpsing only traces of You is like getting love letters but never meeting the loved one, like following footprints along the beach but never catching up with the person who's making them. I need to know for sure that I can really trust You to bring me through this wilderness.

Just one look at Your face would give me more confidence next time people are thirsty and I can't find water. Think what it would do for my credibility—not to mention Yours—if I could stand up in church on Sunday night and tell about the experience. It would strengthen all our faith, increase our ability to relax in Your love. No more doubts. Sounds like a wonderful plan to me, Lord.

Just one look—is that *really* too much to ask? You appeared to others. You showed up in a room without even coming through the door.[5] Then the absentee Thomas declared he wasn't buying the story: "Unless I see the nail marks in his hands and put my finger where the nails were, and put my hand into his side, I will not believe it." You walked into the same house where You'd been the night before, passed through the same walls, and held out Your hands once again: "Put your finger here; see my hands. Reach out your hand and put it into my side. [Thomas,] stop doubting and believe."[6]

You understand about doubts. You know when my faith is so faint it doesn't even show up on the monitor. You know when it's time for a healthy dose of tangible evidence. How faith soars when I can put my fingers on the nail scars, touch Your side where the sword went through. How easy to believe when You show up in the room without using the door. How confidently I can move into my future when I have proof that You are alive and in the business of giving signs.

Today I sit in a room without any doors. I wait

for You to pass through the walls. You came once; I'm certain You will come again.

I've sat in this room now for a good many years, waiting for the sighting. Oh, yes, You *have* appeared to me in other rooms in other ways. I have not been without Your reassurances from time to time. I've seen Your hand moving the pieces on the chessboard of life. You have often orchestrated the details of my life so that I can't help but exclaim, "There is no way I could have brought it all together like that. What a God of love!"

But Lord, those rooms were not *this* room. I need for You to pass through *these* walls, show up in *this* place. I need to see You *here* — in this specific situation, in this specific way. My need is not in the room across the hall, so even if You do show up there, I'll still be waiting for You here.

The sun rises and sets. Days pass. Then months, then years, and still You do not appear in this room. I have devised my plans, followed all necessary steps, reviewed and revised and hoped again. I have thrown away my plans. Wadded them up and pitched them into the waste can. I have said, "Okay, Lord, forget my plans! Do it Your way . . . any way . . . it doesn't even matter how. But *do it*, Lord. Pass through these walls."

"Those who wait for the LORD will gain new strength."[7] Think how strong I am by now. I guess waiting for You to appear is not all bad. It adds dimension to my love. Gives me time to think. Keeps me on my knees. Makes me sensitive to all the others who sit in rooms without doors and wait for You to come through the walls.

But this day I am *not* stronger because of the

waiting. I am weaker. I am hungry and have no bread. You do not move through the crowd handing out rolls. I'm tired of this place. You don't set the bush on fire and give me my marching orders. There is no sighting. No passing through walls. Things do not change. Nothing will change unless You intervene.

I have no doubt You can show Yourself if You choose. But apparently, You do not choose. I sit alone in my room. I read my books and try to believe You are love. You don't show. I pray and try to believe You are love. You don't show. I hear others testify to how You came to them, and I try to believe You are love. You don't show. I ask for the cup to pass from me. You don't show.

You don't take the cup; You give it, even as it is passed down the row in the worship service. "This is my body given for you. . . . This cup is the new covenant in my blood, which is poured out for you."[8]

I take the cup of juice. I drink the symbol of Jesus' blood. " 'Father, if you are willing, take this cup from me; yet not my will, but yours be done. . . . Father, into your hands I commit my spirit.' When he had said this, he breathed his last."[9] You did not show up to take His cup from Him either.

You do not take it from me. In fact, today, You do not even show up. But the cup, the one You did not remove for Your only beloved Son, speaks to me, as I drink the juice and put the empty container in the rack in front of me. . . .

I do not always remove the bitter cup. I asked My Son to drink it. I allowed the cross to be pounded

into the ground, the iron spikes to be driven through His flesh and bone. The epitaph, "This is Jesus, The King of the Jews," was written.[10]

Sometimes, My child, the dream will die and I will not appear before the burial. But whether or not I appear has nothing to do with My love. It has everything to do with the fact that I am God. I do not explain bitter cups, wooden crosses, silent skies. I do not explain My seeming nonintervention. I don't always "intervene" on your behalf because I am God and My love for you goes far beyond removing cups, filling breadbaskets, and showing up in rooms with locked doors.

I know about your need for visible love. Remember? I created you. I know how eagerly you look for signs, collect them and store them in your treasure box.

I know how hard it is for you to live without the evidence of love, visual person that you are. I know you like notes, surprise packages tied up with ribbon, phone calls during the day when you don't expect them. I know about your need for a presence, for someone to sit next to, for a hand to hold. Your love is human. I'm not surprised by your desire for proximity.

But don't be surprised when My love doesn't look like yours. I don't always write love notes, pile the gifts high around your Christmas tree, call home in the middle of the day. Sometimes My love for you is so great it can't be reduced to evidence. Sometimes My love is best communicated by giving you room to trust Me. I don't always rush to the aid of My loved ones. Sometimes, the very situation in which it seems I am doing nothing at all for you is when I am really doing the most.

You're right—sometimes I do show up on grassy knolls and fill breadbaskets to overflowing. I care about empty stomachs.

But you heard Me sigh after I gave you bread. Sometimes, child, I am sad about the way you love Me. You followed Me across the lake not because you saw past the sign to who I really am, but because "you ate the loaves and had your fill."[11] The danger with miracles is that after a while you want Me for what I can do for you rather than for who I am. I do not always fill breadbaskets. Full baskets are not proof of My love. In fact, greater proof may be that I choose not to fill them.

Do not seek My miracles—seek *Me*. Forget about what I can do for you and concentrate on who I am—loving, just, patient, faithful, forgiving. Do not worry about how I will convince the unbelieving world if they have no sign. My ways of convincing are not always tangible. Forget about strengthening your faith because I show up for you dressed in miracles. Actually, your faith will grow stronger through believing Me when there are no signs than through believing when there are.

Yes, there will be times when I let you see where the nails went through. Sometimes I will stand so close you can put your hands where the sword pierced My side. But blessed are those who have not seen and yet have believed.[12] Sometimes I will pass through walls and stand in your midst. But oh, how much better for our love had you never doubted Me, had you been willing to believe My love whether you saw My nail scars or not.

What it all comes down to is this: Are you

willing to live without the evidence? Can you sit on the cleft in the rock, let Me cover you with My hand, while My glory passes by?[13] Are you willing to settle for a view of My back when you've asked to see My face? Are you content to take My love as I choose to give it, rather than as you want it given?

I love you whether I show you My face or not. I love you whether you enter the promised land or not. I know it is not your kind of love that would leave an old man to die alone on the gloomy crags of Mount Nebo, when I had promised him a home west of the Jordan.[14]

Some would not call it love when, for one impulsive act of disobedience, I banished My servant from the promised land, condemning him to live the rest of his life with an unfulfilled longing for home.[15]

Some sign of love, you think, to make an old man labor up a mountain and gaze on the home he will never inhabit but gave most of his life to gain for his people.

No, it did not look like love that day when I did not show up for Moses on Mount Nebo. But it *was* love. My final act of love was to bury him among the mountain crags. And his epitaph read: Here lies Moses. "No prophet has risen in Israel like Moses, whom the LORD knew face to face, who did all those miraculous signs and wonders the LORD sent him to do in Egypt. . . . For no one has ever shown the mighty power or performed the awesome deeds that Moses did in the sight of all Israel."[16]

My child, I love *you*, even as I loved Moses. You must never forget that My love is always with you, whether it looks like it or not. You must believe it. Say it to yourself three, four, five times a day—"*He loves me,* whether I see His love or not." Write it in your journal, tell it to your children and your friends, live confidently and joyfully, as though you *do* see evidence of My love.

And if I ever seem to leave you alone on a lonely mountain crag, where you cannot see traces of My love, look back to those experiences in which you did see traces. Do what Moses did when he found out the promised land would never be home. When he could not thank Me for the present, he thanked Me for the past:

> Remember the days of old; consider the
> generations long past . . . when the Most
> High gave the nations their inheritance. . . .
> In a desert land he found [Israel], in a bar-
> ren and howling waste. He shielded him
> and cared for him; he guarded him as the
> apple of his eye, like an eagle that stirs
> up its nest and hovers over its young, that
> spreads its wings to catch them and car-
> ries them on its pinions. The LORD alone
> led him.[17]

If I choose not to show Myself in the room where you wait for Me, remember all the other rooms where I *have* met you. Thank Me for those other rooms of visitation.

But you must even come to the place where you can thank Me for the walls I have *not* passed through. For until you can thank Me for rooms not visited, lands never possessed, faces never seen, cups never removed, you have not trusted *Me* at all. If you cannot thank Me for the signs I never gave, you have not thanked Me at all.

And when you have learned to live without miracles, you will awaken one day and find that *you* are the miracle. You will not be frantic for signs, so sure of My love will you be. You will not need visible tokens along the way. If those tokens should come, you will be humbled and grateful, but you will not live and love by signs alone.

When you have learned to live without miracles, you will not try to manipulate My love, like a child whining for attention. You will not pout when I don't "show up." You will not play the martyr role—"See how much I do without." *You will not try to tell Me how to love you.*

Then you will trust Me enough to let Me love you in My own way—whether tangible or not. You will not demand a sign. You will let Me come and go as I please. And even if I should deny you a sign, you will not accuse, "You don't love me anymore!" You will be gracious and cheerful. "He loves me whether I see proof or not, whether He is here in this room, holding my hand or not." You will be steady, for your security is not in signs (which may come and go) but in My love (which is forever).

I know you are sitting there in your room, My child, waiting for My intervention. I love you even as you sit there waiting for Me to come in the way you think I should come. My question to you is this: If I never choose to pass through those walls, would you trust Me just as much? Love Me just as much? Be just as sure of My love?

I love you even as you sit there in worship, drinking the cup, eating the bread, remembering My blood and My body, which was broken for you. I offer you no spectacular visions. Today I offer you *Myself*—My body, My blood, My love. Oh, that it would be enough for you. . . .

The house of worship is quiet. My room of waiting is quiet. My thoughts are quiet. I see the wafer—His body, broken for me. I taste the cup—His blood, poured out for me.

> *He was wounded for [my] transgressions,*
> *He bore [my] sins in His body on the tree;*
> *For [my] guilt He gave [me] peace,*
> *From [my] bondage gave release,*
> *And with His stripes, and with His stripes,*
> *And with His stripes [my] soul [is] healed.*[18]

Lord, You posted Your sign of love two thousand years ago, Your body nailed to a crossbeam outside of Jerusalem while the skies darkened and the earth shuddered. Forgive me for wanting more.

Forgive me for eating the miracle bread on a grassy knoll one day, and then expecting a refill. Forgive me for demanding to see Your face, for insisting You come through walls. Forgive me for asking that love signs be posted every ten feet—and for pouting when they don't appear.

Forgive me for closing doors on Your love when I feel ignored, for playing the heroine who shouts to the world how noble it is living the austere life where love does not drip from every chandelier. Forgive me for trying to program Your love.

I give it up, Lord, this need to see love, this burdensome expectancy that waits with Thomas for You to show Your hands and Your side. If I never put my hands on Your nail scars, never touch the place where the sword pierced Your side, it is okay, Lord. Today it is okay. I fold my blueprints. I cap my pen. My plans for seeing evidence are over — here today I declare them null and void.

You posted Your love sign once — in a terribly visible way, for all the world to see. I will return to that sign, Lord. I will cling to its shadow. The cross was the greatest evidence of love that could ever be given. How did I so soon forget?

As I walk from the place of worship, I leave more than a church service. I leave a room of waiting, a room of unfulfilled desires and what seems like unanswered prayer. You have not passed through the walls to come to me. But miracle of miracles, today I pass through the walls and come to You with no expectations. I return to the cross. Here I will remember how much I am loved, accepting Your love, given in Your way.

> Lord, I see no trace of You today.
> The morning rains, the skies rumble,
> the work piles high.
> Nothing has changed,
> even after my bedtime prayer last night.
>
> If only I knew where to find You —
> if only I could run to Your arms
> hear Your quiet voice above the rumble,

see Your gentle face through the storm,
know You are hard at work answering my
prayer.

But the sky thunders on
the rains keep coming,
and You seem nowhere to be found . . .
not within eyesight,
not within earshot.
The phone rings into empty air:
no answer . . . no answer . . . no answer.

It is a morning
to stand before my mirror
look into my own eyes and say,
"He loves me,
even though it seems
He is nowhere to be found."

NOTES
 1. Mark 8:1-12.
 2. Mark 8:12.
 3. Mark 8:12.
 4. Exodus 33:18.
 5. John 20:19.
 6. John 20:24-27.
 7. Isaiah 40:31, NASB.
 8. Luke 22:19-20.
 9. Luke 22:42, 23:46.
10. John 19:19.
11. John 6:26.
12. John 20:29.
13. Exodus 33:18-23.
14. Deuteronomy 34:1-8.
15. Numbers 20:1-12.
16. Deuteronomy 34:10-12.
17. Deuteronomy 32:7-12.
18. From the hymn "He Was Wounded for Our Transgressions" by
    Thomas O. Chisholm and Merrill Dunlap, 1941.

5

I CAN'T MAKE SENSE OF LIFE
The Longing for Understanding

here is a strange note in the wind tonight. It rumbles through the firs like a freight train gone wild, careening out of control at breakneck speed to who knows where, dragging along with it who knows what.

I wrap my robe tighter around me, peer from the window into the darkened fury. The ancient oak in our front yard waves and bows in all directions. The trees are taking a beating. The world, it seems, is taking a beating—bent and bruised by forces it does not understand or like.

I do not understand this wind. But even on calmer days, when I lift my face to cool breezes on a hot summer afternoon or with pleasure guide my kite along updrafts on a balmy March day, I still do not understand the wind. I do not know its source, cannot chart or predict its course. It is a commodity I cannot explain, contain, or describe, for I have never seen it. It moves as it will, does what it will, rises and falls far above or below my feeble attempts to comprehend.

I stand tonight at the mercy of what I do not understand and cannot predict. Even the weather experts are not attempting to explain the wild creature that has ridden into town, unannounced and unexpected. "Wait and see" is the best they can offer to reassure a nervous public who peer out their windows in alarm at the freight train that rampages through their yards. No one knows. No one understands. No one can name, much less tame, the wind. We are left to flounder in speculation and, at best, calculated miscalculations.

But oh, how we work at our calculations.

For every wind that blows, we must have a category—draft, zephyr, breeze, squall, sheer, hurricane, tornado, cyclone, typhoon, trade wind. For every movement of air, there must be direction—point of the compass, cardinal points, half points, quarter points; north, east, south, west, north by east, east by northeast, northeast by north. For every breeze there must be an instrument of measurement—weather vane, anemometer, wind scale, windsock. And still the unseen invader sneaks into town, takes us by surprise, and leaves the forecasters speechless.

Lord, I'm bothered by unseen invaders sneaking into town, running rampage. I fear what cannot be controlled and predicted. I am uneasy when there are no words to describe. I am confused by lack of category, worried when there are no precise instruments of measurement. How do I understand the wind if I cannot explain, describe, measure, predict?

How do I understand *You* and love if I cannot explain, describe, measure, predict? You are above, below, around, coming and going *from* wherever You will *to* wherever You will. Doing whatever You will along the way—silent, unseen. No need to show Yourself directly, only Your effects. No need to explain Yourself above and beyond Your written Word. No need to defend Your actions or describe Your plan so that Your children will understand.

You operate independently. Your independence is what makes You God, above and beyond us. Your independence is also what makes it hard for me to understand Your workings and Your ways. Sometimes, when I don't understand Your ways, I don't understand Your love. And sometimes when I don't understand Your love, I close the door on it.

My world closes its doors on love if it does not understand. "I will never understand you!" Slam the door on dialogue. "Irreconcilable differences." Slam the door on marriage. "You and I are on two different wavelengths." Slam the door on teenagers. "We're just two different personalities." Slam the door on friendship. "I don't understand, Lord!" Slam the door on Your love.

Bumping against closed doors is the human impulse to understand and to be understood. We are frustrated in relationships when we are not able to do both. So deep is the pain when our attempts are thwarted. It is often easier to close the door and walk away. Sometimes no love is better than a love we don't understand.

I want You to understand me, dear Lord. *But I also want to understand You.* You created me with reason. Reason begs to be satisfied. I need to figure out my world and how You are working in it. I need to make sense out of nonsense, order the disorder, tuck in the loose ends that are flying wild. I need to name the wind. When I cannot, I cower in my house, peer out at the invader, keep the doors and windows tightly shut. I do not walk into gales I cannot explain.

Sometimes this road You've put me on makes no sense, has no rhyme or reason. The shortest distance between two points is a straight line. You have me traveling circles, roundabouts, detours, going south to eventually get north. Did You forget to check the map before giving me directions? How do I rest in Your love when You have me following nonsense directions, when the wind seems to be blowing at me from all angles, pushing me in crazy patterns?

How do I rest in Your love when You have
given me a reasonable mind for living in an unreasonable world? Why do the righteous suffer? The
innocent die? The servants get stepped on while the
self-centered advance? Why does evil prosper? Why
are the weeds stronger than the grass? Why is work
painful? Why does the wind blow out of control? I
chase after the wind and find no meaning:

> "Meaningless! Meaningless!" says the
> Teacher. "Utterly meaningless! Everything
> is meaningless." What does man gain from
> all his labor at which he toils under the
> sun? All things are wearisome. . . . What
> has been will be again, what has been done
> will be done again; there is nothing new
> under the sun. . . . What a heavy burden
> God has laid on men! I have seen all the
> things that are done under the sun; all of
> them are meaningless, a chasing after the
> wind. . . . I have seen the burden God
> has laid on men. . . . He has also set eter-
> nity in the hearts of men; yet they cannot
> fathom what God has done from beginning
> to end.[1]

The Teacher and I chase after the wind, bent
on finding meaning, reason, understanding of our
world. The search has been on for millennia. It will
go on for another millennium unless time ends — and
forever lays all questions to rest. I am part of the vast
throng who chase after the wind. Why? Why do we
need so badly to understand?

Maybe we are on this perpetual quest because

we are (supposedly) reasonable creatures. Reason is an appetite that must somehow be satisfied — call it curiosity, inquisitiveness, thoughtfulness, inventiveness, creativity, logic.

Maybe we chase after the wind because it is easier to open ourselves to what we understand. We fear what we can't figure out. I will not fling wide my doors or windows to the invader on rampage through my yard. Like the first disciples, I am terrified of what I don't recognize and comprehend. I will not welcome aboard strange forms that walk the dark waves.[2]

I chase after the wind. But the wind is against me, causing the waves to crash, causing me to fear. In my fear, I sit down and discuss what it is I do not understand. One does not commit oneself by mere discussion. In fact, discussion is a clever way to avoid commitment to what we don't understand. What is this strange form walking across the water? Do we have a name for it? A category for it? Has anyone ever seen such a thing before? How does it act? Can it be trusted? What will be the outcome if we open ourselves to it? Should we refer it to a research committee?

As long as I am studying it, writing about it, analyzing it and trying to figure it out, I can keep the door closed — the strange form at arm's length. Analysis is sometimes a subtle way of avoiding love.

Lord, You know how hard it is for me to open the door to what I don't understand. I am full of fear when it comes to the unknown form walking across the water, the strange wind that blows. Sometimes You are that strange wind that blows on me. Just when I think I have found Your wonderful plan for my life, the wind shifts.

Storms that blow our homes and businesses and lives out of order don't make sense. In their wake I try feverishly to restore the order. For my peace of mind. For the health of my spirit. For the sake of something to say. For the sake of Your love for me, dear Lord. Within love is the need to be understood and to understand. I seek to make sense of these jumbles so that I can trust Your love, so that I can open the doors of my spirit.

But long after tonight's storm has passed, I am still caught in a jumble. I am in disarray, even though my house is in order. The dinner dishes are washed, dried, and neatly stacked in the cupboard. Newspapers are properly folded in the brown grocery bag that sits in the broom closet, en route to the recycling bin. The kitchen floor has been swept clean of crumbs. Classical music softens the evening. But strange winds blow again—this time inside my house rather than outside. Tones and overtones I do not understand—cannot understand no matter how hard I try. And tonight I try. I really do try.

The house is in order but my finances are not. My husband and I are not. Discord. We do not understand each other. Differences. Glaring differences forever raising their ugly heads from the little black budget book that lies open on my desk. It is filled with all sorts of confusion. We attempt discussion.

"This is who I am. This is what I need from you when it comes to your expenditures."

"But this is who *I* am and this is what *I* need when it comes to my expenditures. . . . This is how

I was raised . . . this is how I see it . . . this is what I feel. . . ."

"I don't understand. I don't know where you're coming from, and I sure can't tell where you're going here on these lined pages. . . ."

Discussion. Concessions. But still the differences. More discussion. More concessions. But always the differences. We work into the night, each of us trying, really trying. Finally we close the budget book. Crisis averted. But still the differences. Still I don't understand him. Still he doesn't understand me. And then, Lord, as though You've ridden into town on that strange wind again, in my own voice, I hear Yours.

"Well, honey, I know you don't always understand me. Don't even try. Just keep loving me. I guess you don't have to understand me to love me. . . ."

I don't often hear You speak when I'm jumbled in budget books, but tonight I do.

I hear Your voice, dear Lord, as surely as if You were here, closing the book with me. . . .

Child, don't try to understand Me. Just love Me. Just let Me love you. You don't have to understand Me to open yourself to My love.

You're right — I do ride the wild winds into town sometimes. I do appear in forms you have never seen, sound notes you have never heard. This makes you wonder if I get My signals crossed, if I take you south in order to get you north. I seem to have plopped you down, reasonable creature that you are, into an unreasonable world. You do not understand all this because I am God and you are you.

May I remind you how different we really are? You are human; I am divine. You are finite; I am infinite. You need love; I delight in love but do not need it. You need to be understood; I am above the need to be understood. You cannot understand; I understand perfectly. You are of time; I am of eternity. You are of reason; I am above reason. You are blown by the wind; I blow the wind.

For now, you'll have to live with our differences and be content not to understand Me because of them. They are the very things that set Me apart as the Holy One—God with you, but God above you. "As the heavens are higher than the earth, so are my ways higher than your ways and my thoughts than your thoughts."[3] If I were not different from you, you could not worship and respect Me.

You will need to forget about understanding Me for My sake. I do not need to be understood. You will also need to forget about understanding Me for *your* sake. You do not need to make sense of Me. To know Me? Yes. To understand Me? No. You will have to be content simply to know that I understand you. That will have to be enough for now.

The truth of the matter is, My child, I cannot be reduced to formula. "As you do not know the path of the wind, or how the body is formed in a mother's womb, so you cannot understand the work of God, the Maker of all things."[4] Your human mind will never be able to completely understand the things of the spirit. "The wind blows wherever it pleases. You hear its sound, but you cannot tell where it comes from or where it is going. So it is with everyone born of the Spirit."[5]

What I do in My world will never completely make sense to you. That is why you must say to yourself, three, four, five times a day: "*I do not understand, but He does.* I do not need to understand in order to love Him, to know that He loves me."

My answers will not always be there for you (in fact, they usually aren't). My ways will not always make sense to you (in fact, they usually won't). Sometimes My paths do go in circles, follow the roundabouts, go south to get north. Sometimes My paths dead-end against an old fence-post sign that reads, "No Trespassing. Keep Out." You will think, "But the route was so clear, so straight, so well-marked!" Driving down a four-lane highway into a dead end will not make sense to you.

It did not make sense to Paul, either, as he packed his bags for what he thought would be a trip to Asia.[6] The map was spread out before him on his nightstand. The candlelight was strong. No misreading of the red and blue lines, no doubts about the route. Asia or bust. But the border guards said no. I said no. Paul's path dead-ended against an old fence-post sign that read, "No Trespassing. Keep out."

So what do you do when it seems as if I took you on a wrong turn to nowhere? Spend a day in a motel in seclusion rereading the map? Fast and pray for a week so that you might understand what went wrong? Form a committee to study the theology of closed doors and dead ends? Put Me under a microscope to try to figure out how I strategize missionary trips?

Oh, My child, when you come up against the dead-end signs, don't try to unscramble My plan. Come into My presence and let Me love you. Rest in My love and you will be reassured that My plan is loving, even though it makes no sense.

Then you won't be paralyzed by apparent wrong turns. You will forget Asia for the time being, get a good night's rest, wake with the sun to a new vision, and head out in a new direction. Perhaps later the trip will make sense, perhaps never. But you will keep moving, surrounded by My love, confident in My ability to keep My creation on track. You will know whom you have believed, and will be convinced that I am able to guard what you have entrusted to Me for My ultimate outcome.[7]

So what if your path doesn't make sense? Be assured that *I* know the way you take. I have planned your route. I alone know the highways, the back roads and the interstates, the detours and the muddy ruts. When the paths seem to tangle, I still hold the map.

Child, surrender your need to understand. Make it your goal to love Me rather than to understand Me. Put away your microscope; I can't be contained on a slide anyway. I am not a species to be analyzed, categorized, and filed neatly in its proper place.

I want you to look to Me — not to scrutinize Me, but to *enjoy* Me. When you can't speak the language of the strange wind that blows, don't try to break the code. Simply enjoy the sounds. When you can't figure out why you're sitting on the ash

heap, even though your friends jump to explanations, don't waste your energy asking why.

I will not answer your "why," but I will
speak to you out of the storm.[8] I will say, "Don't
try to figure Me out, just look at Me—look at what
I can do, and then love Me. Trust Me, not because
I explain Myself to you, but because I am God, the
Creator of your world."

You are not foolish in your attempts to
understand your world, to make sense out of
life—only human. My creation has been trying
to figure out its Creator for centuries. You are but
part of the quest. I do not hold it against you. I
only remind you that peace will come not when
you figure Me out, but when you open yourself
to My love. Your peace will come when you rest in
Me rather than in My answers for you.

So come to Me as the child you are. Children, though they do ask Me why (and so will you),
come to Me to crawl up on My lap and be near Me.
They come to Me for love, not answers. If you come
for answers, you will go away sad. If you come for
love, you will be filled. To know the love of God,
which surpasses all understanding[9]—that is what
I desire for you.

Sometimes life will not make sense to you.
You will chase after the wind and find nothing.
Don't be alarmed: It doesn't mean there is nothing
there. It only means you must see this topsy-turvy
world through eyes of faith. If your world has to
make sense before you open yourself to My love,
you will never do it. The greater side of faith is
to open yourself to love even when love does not
make sense.

Don't go chasing after an ordered world. It will not be ordered until eternity; therefore, it will not make sense until eternity. But in your quest to find meaning, you will find *Me*. I will be standing there in the midst of the chaos, holding out My arms of love. Through the scattered shapes of a thousand-piece jigsaw puzzle that defy your efforts to fit them together, you will find Me, patiently waiting for you.

When you find Me, you will discover that meaning springs not from being able to solve the puzzle, but from receiving My love. You will be so glad to see Me, you will open those closed doors of your spirit that you slammed shut in fear when you could not figure things out. You will let Me love you again. The answers won't matter. Answers don't matter when you are absorbed in love. When you are secure in My love, you can stop chasing the wind. You can put the puzzle away and go to bed. You are loved. You do not need to understand.

As you find satisfaction in My love, you will find satisfaction in your world. You will not need to worry about naming the seasons of your life, as filled with extremes as they are. You will find that "there is a time for everything, and a season for every activity under heaven."[10] You will rest in the assurance that I have "made everything beautiful in its time,"[11] and that everything I do "will endure forever; nothing can be added to it and nothing taken from it."[12]

When you open yourself to My love rather than struggle to understand it, you will have laid aside a heavy burden. You will seldom reflect on the days of your life, because I will keep you occupied with gladness of heart.[13]

When you open the doors to My love again, you will find peace. You will hear a familiar voice coming to you over the waves. True, what you do not understand will frighten you for a moment—"It is a ghost!" Yes, you will fear the wind. But when you hear the voice, so dear and so reassuring will it be, that you will come to Me. I will come to you. Love will meet there in mid-lake, even as the boat rocks in towering waves.

You will have your shaky moments. You will doubt; I will have to pull you out of the water. You will not understand how to walk on water or how to trust Me completely.

But you will welcome Me on board. And when you do, *the wind will die down.* You will recognize Me for who I am: "Truly you are the Son of God."[14] You will know how great is My love for you. But you will have no idea how I calm the wind; you will not even try to figure it out. My child, when you are secure in My love, how I take care of the wind will not even matter to you.

The soft evening music calls us to rest. We put away the little black budget book, clear the desk of calculator, scratch paper, pencils, empty envelopes, and written checks.

The unpaid bill file is still partially full. Not every line in the budget book has been unscrambled. The differences in how we view finances are still as different as my brown eyes from his blue ones. He still does not understand me completely. I still do not understand him completely.

After our evening cup of tea, we get ready for bed and turn out the light.

"I love you," he whispers through the dark.

"I love you too," I whisper back.

We drift into sleep. There is no doubt about our love. I go to sleep with my own words ringing in my ears. "You don't have to understand me to love me."

During the night, I hear the wind begin to stir through the firs again. I wake, give momentary thought to the unrest that appears to be brewing. I am loved by the One who stirs the winds. I have no inclination to get up, peer into the dark to try to make sense of what is happening. I return to peaceful sleep. Dear Lord, I return to Your love. I release my need to understand.

> *As long as*
> *you are not me*
> *and I am not you,*
> *I will not completely understand*
> *why you respond to some things the way you do.*
> *What you mean by what you say,*
> *why you do the things you do,*
> *how to interpret the look on your face.*
>
> *You are you.*
> *And . . . I am me.*
> *I chose you because of it.*
> *Opened wide my heart*
> *to love and be loved*
> *by someone not like me.*

How quickly our differences
can become walls.
Our lack of understanding
becomes a closed door.
But our love is different.
Because . . . even when we don't understand,
we keep opening the doors
and coming back for more.

NOTES
1. Ecclesiastes 1:2-3,8-9,13-14; 3:10-11.
2. Matthew 14:22-33.
3. Isaiah 55:9.
4. Ecclesiastes 11:5.
5. John 3:8.
6. Acts 16:6-8.
7. 2 Timothy 1:12.
8. Job 38:1.
9. Ephesians 3:19.
10. Ecclesiastes 3:1.
11. Ecclesiastes 3:11.
12. Ecclesiastes 3:14.
13. Ecclesiastes 5:20.
14. Matthew 14:33.

6
I FEAR THE COLD
The Longing for Renewal

rom the harbor of the ancient city of Ephesus, mighty ships once sailed to sea. Ephesus — proud city of Asia Minor, gateway for trade, host to rich caravans from wealthy civilizations. Life once bred on its shores, pulsed through its temples, its theaters, its columned porticoes, thronged into its vast basilica. Thousands came to worship at its shrine — temple of the goddess Artemis, one of the seven wonders of the ancient world, four times the size of Athens' Parthenon.

Ephesus: strong, powerful. Influence radiated from its hub like shock waves from the epicenter of an earthquake. What Ephesus felt, the surrounding world felt. What the proconsul at Ephesus said, the whole province of Asia Minor did. What the Ephesians championed, the world worshiped. There could be little doubt about vibrancy of life there. No one dreamed that such life would ever die.

But it did. Slowly. Gradually. Unnoticed at first, silent forces began to nibble away at the city's life. Winds and rains took the topsoil. Eager merchants stripped away timber and charcoal. Silt, sand, and sludge crept down the hinterlands and began to choke the harbor. When the harbor began to die, the city began to die. When the city began to die, the church of Ephesus began to die.

The creeping death gained entrance through the port, moved inward — into the soul and spirit of the invincible city, into the soul and spirit of the church. "I hold this against you," wrote the prophet John to the church at Ephesus: "You have forsaken your first love."[1] Jesus' prediction had indeed begun to come true — "Because of the increase of wickedness, the love of most will grow cold."[2]

Deterioration carried out its work. Over the centuries, the hills slid into the sea, and polluted harbor turned to swamp. Ships set their sails for other ports. Merchants ran out of goods to sell. Temples stood deserted. Brick and mortar fell to the battering elements. Marbled avenues began to heave and burst open, like bubbles in a boiling pot; columns crumbled. Civilization chose a more fertile plain. Finally, all that was left of Ephesus were broken bits of faded glory. Today birds lay eggs in her swamp and buzzards circle her dead carcass.

I stand today among the rubble of an Ephesus of sorts. I see the effects of a love grown cold. I walk through the silence of deserted streets, stand among ruins, and recall the days when life acted itself out in great theaters, echoed in marbled halls. I see an infested swamp and think, *Great ships used to sail from this place and transport life to the world.*

There is something tragic about a great city that strangles itself on neglect and distraction. There is something sad about love grown cold, about freshness gone tired and stale. Something painful about vibrancy turned to dissipation.

This creeping cold is a scary thought, Lord. If strong civilizations can gradually petrify and die from lack of attention, what might happen when love is not kept fresh? When love grows cold, I suppose most anything can happen. Ephesus is proof.

Sometimes I hold back from love when it is offered because I see visions of Ephesus. I don't reach eagerly for fresh love because someday I might have to stand among rubble with only memories of when love was new. I don't want to look out on a swamp and be reminded of my own neglect. Sometimes, it seems, the worst pain of all is the knowledge that you have let love grow cold. Perhaps it is the threat of staleness that causes me to close the door on love.

What worsens the threat is that I feel responsible for the harbor. Keeping love fresh is hard work. What if I commit the sin of neglect? What if I become distracted? Blind to little things? Insensitive? Preoccupied with building magnificence? What if I do not notice that grain by grain, silt and sand are gradually choking my port? What if I get so busy that marble and brick become deserted shells? And Lord, if our love grows cold, it will not be Your affection for me that has cooled. It will be mine for You.

Sometimes the memories of freshness are haunting because they remind me of decline. I remember what once was. I remember great bursts of joy and enthusiasm for love and life. I knelt at the altar with great visions of vibrancy. Life would never again be stale and stagnant. Fresh love would pour into all my mornings like the early sun streaming into my bedroom window. I would keep the harbor clean, the ground soft so the seed could grow. I would work the soil every day. I would keep my heart soft so that love could grow and mature and spread until all my world could taste of love that grew fresh from my tree. I would move on wings for the rest of my life.

But Lord, *how quickly great bursts lose their steam*. How soon the cares of the world crowd in and steal the eternal quality of love. The weeds grow up and choke the seed. Sometimes I am so full of the mundane I have no thoughts of love anymore.

I think no further than what needs doing this very moment. Beds to make. Dishes to wash. Weeds to pull. Paperwork to finish. I think not of where I am going in this love of ours, but of where I am — stuck with daily routine. How do I get the dryer running again when its motor goes out? What do I do about the water softener in the basement that is giving out strange sounds of neglect? How do I get this assignment done by the deadline?

I have no time to maintain the harbor when I must meet deadlines, keep the dryer running. There's no room for thinking sublime thoughts of love when I'm cleaning out the crud that's clogging the water softener. One grain of sand at a time, the silt builds up in the port of Ephesus. The weeds grow. And most of the time, I don't even notice.

When love is neglected, it stagnates. Polite formalities soon replace spontaneous tenderness and careful attention. I am proper, thoughtful, and dutiful. I perform with great care what the unwritten contract calls for. Remember birthdays. Iron those all-cotton shirts. Fix a favorite pie. Say "I love you" once, twice, maybe even three times a day. Show up in church, once, twice, maybe even three times a week. Give my tithe. Write to the missionaries. Take casseroles to the sick. Polite formalities of love fill my time; they do not fill my spirit. Weeds grow in untended spirits. Empty harbors breed swamps.

I sense stagnation when all I can talk to You about is the weather. "It's raining on my child. Please deliver her from the storm. It's raining on me. Please take me to a sunnier climate." I sense stagnation when I will not venture beyond the shallows in my communication with You. I'll tell You what I have done today, but please don't ask why I've seemed silent and distracted recently. I'll give You the run-down on who I saw and what she said and how it goes with her daughter who just left for the mission field of South America. Oh yes, and I will ask You to please bless her daughter who just left for the mission field of South America.

But let's not get in too deep here — into stale-ness of soul or why the harbor fills with silt. If we don't talk about it, perhaps it will go away. And sometimes silence, as painful as it may be, is not nearly so painful as discourse that explores tender places of the soul. Besides, exploring tender places of the soul takes time — at least an hour to get into and more than an hour to get out of. It takes less time not to talk.

Here, I'll make You a pot of coffee — but let's postpone conversation for a little while, okay? Right now there's a dryer to fix. A file to organize. A manuscript to complete. Time with You is impor-tant, Lord — but couldn't we do it *next* week? I do want to talk to You about my fears, but we need blocks of time — like the three months of summer vacation. "We'll get together then, Lord. I know we'll have a good time then."

I wonder — is my love cooling off because it seems I don't need You as much as I used to? I've built my city with careful plan and thought. I've invested wisely; years have added maturity and strength. I've climbed some pretty steep moun-tains — excuse me, You and I have climbed some pretty steep mountains. It was Your arm I leaned on all the way up.

Sure, we've weathered pretty severe storms

together. It was Your hand I held onto when the winds were so strong they could have blown me apart. But right now there's a lull. I feel strong, serene, in balance. I feel capable, self-assured.

But then, Lord, so did Ephesus. *Ephesus*: one of the seven wonders of the ancient world. *Ephesus*: strong, invincible, self-assured. *Ephesus*: stone-cold ruins of a faded love.

Is it a sign of creeping coldness to stop needing one another? Is my independence driving us apart? Are my capabilities keeping me from leaning on Your arm, from taking Your hand? Has my strength become my own worst enemy?

"Here, My child, let Me help you."

"But Lord, *I can do it by myself.*"

And You, dear Father, are left out in the cold.

Then, too, I wonder about familiarity. Does my love begin to stagnate when I get too used to feeling like I've known You all my life? You are my comfortable old slippers waiting by the fireplace. Nothing new. Nothing exciting. Just the same old slippers — but oh, how soothing to tired feet.

Now there *is* something to be said for comfortable love that doesn't always need an exciting plot to carry it along. It plods along on its own — steady, sure, something I can always count on.

But frankly, comfortable love sometimes loses its luster. I wake up in the morning to shades of gray and brown and long lists of things to do and not enough time to do them all and an endless repetition of last week's cycle. Same old news on the radio, just wrapped in a different broadcast set on a different continent. You are here, easing me through it all, but You can be as gray to me as the sky. As brown as the winter grass. As uneventful as the news.

Yes, it's comforting to know You're nearby.
I'm grateful to have been forgiven, redeemed, recre-
ated in Your righteousness. But even the doctrine of
it all sometimes lacks luster. I memorize Your words,
hide them in my heart that I might not sin against
You.[3] But Lord, I confess I know You so well I almost
feel that I know what You're thinking. I sing Your
songs of praise. But You are a song I know so well,
I don't even have to think about the words. You're
just *there*, like the ground and sky and air. That's
comforting. But it's also frightening.

What's frightening about it? *I remember how
different new love was.* I remember when he was the
first thing on my mind in the morning. I remember
that I couldn't wait to start the day because it held
possibilities of getting to know him better. I remember when closeness was everything. I remember how
I went out of my way just to walk by his dormitory
window. How I loved to sit close to him, arm touching arm. How I carried his smile with me all through
the day and read his letters over and over in the halls
between classes. I remember when others could see
love on my face. "Your eyes are shining. You've been
with him again!"

I remember how love used to energize me,
no matter how mundane and ordinary the task. I
dusted and mopped classroom floors and thought
about him. I studied French and English and theology and thought about him. There was always
plenty of room for him in my thoughts, my schedule,
my life.

When love was fresh I walked not in fantasy
but in wonder. I wonder what he's doing. I wonder

what he's thinking. I wonder how he's feeling. I wonder what he dreams about. I wonder if he's missing me.

I also wondered in amazement. He notices me. He cares about me. Out of all the women on this campus block, he has chosen me. Out of all the women in the world, he has chosen me. I wonder why.

Sadly to say, Lord, I don't wonder as much anymore. I don't even think to ask wonder questions. I don't stand and gaze on Your works of art and say, "He planted that tree. He poured that lake. He painted that flower. He loves me. Isn't He amazing!"

I don't notice as many details about You anymore. I forget to stop and look at the loving touches You leave all over my life and my world. Messages that once read, "I love you, Ruth. I'm glad you're Mine." Sometimes I even forget to open the envelope. I forget to watch for Your smile, to notice what You are doing, to feel when You might be disappointed.

Sometimes I don't go to sleep at night with a sense of pleasure at Your nearness. Instead, I go to sleep irritated at Your loud snoring. Yes — sometimes, dear Lord, I even think of You as an inconvenience. You're keeping me from something. Is this what happens when love grows stale?

I wonder, Lord, did the Ephesians walk through a city grown so familiar that after a while they stopped noticing how the marble shone in the sunlight? Where they too busy trying to create beauty to notice Your beauty that was already there? Did they cram so many tasks into their daily routines that they simply squeezed You out of their days, their schedules, their hearts?

I seem mired in the swamp. Its decay is seeping into my sense of love. It hasn't felt fresh in a long, long time. I drink stale water, breathe stale air. Move in and out of my days on time, but not on wings. The harbor is filling up with silt.

But today, I do not sit by the harbor. I sit by a freshwater lake that is fed by some unseen spring. I have not come to seek renewal, only a few minutes of peace and quiet away from the traffic that races around this natural haven in the middle of town. I have not come to notice, at least not intentionally. I have come just to sit and to rest my feet. I have no expectation for refreshment, only the hope that I will make it back to work on time.

But Lord, how like You to show up even when I'm not expecting You. How like You to break through stale ground with a new bud when spring is not yet official, to water parched grass with fresh dew when the weather forecast says "no rain."

I watch as a city work crew, dressed in green, rakes under the spruce and pine that line the lake, trims dead branches from the maples and oaks, gathers winter's debris and stuffs it into large brown bags. I think, as I watch them hard at work, of how much they enhance the beauty of this place.

Then, as clearly as if You are speaking through one of the green-clad gardeners I am watching, I hear Your voice. . . .

Look at this lake, child. It's peaceful. It's fresh. Its waters are clear.

This lake did not get that way because of the city maintenance crew. This lake is fresh because of the underground spring that feeds it. True, the workers enhance the beauty and keep rubble out of the water, but I renew its freshness with My unseen spring. I am the Keeper of the lake.

Today you are in need of renewal. You are tired of the cold. You are remembering how it was when love was new. And you are feeling a long, long way from those days.

You have become paranoid about Ephesus, preoccupied with decline. You are worried about maintenance as though vibrancy depends solely upon your efforts. But the life of the harbor at Ephesus depended more upon deep-rooted trees that would keep topsoil from eroding and washing into its waters than it did on those who dredged its silt.

Learn from Ephesus, but do not let it haunt you. I give you visual illustrations, not to paralyze you in fear but to lead you into growth. Your efforts to tend the harbor do not make it fresh. I feed the lakes and seas with freshness by underground streams and river outlets. I alone bring the cool, clear waters.

You are in need of freshness. Keep your eye on the harbor, yes—be aware of neglects and distractions—but focus on putting your roots down deep into the rich soil of My love. Let Me love you. You need only come to Me and draw from the silent spring. I will refresh you.

I am the new life you seek. "I have come that [you] may have life, and have it to the full."[4] I died for the sake of new life and I rose for the sake of new life. I have made you a new creation so that you could live a new life.[5] I offered you a new covenant—a new life for us together.[6]

I am always making all things new, whether it be things past, present, or future. My love is always new. I pour My mercies out on you fresh every morning, like the manna I dropped every day to My children in the wilderness. Because of My great love, you are not consumed, for My compassions never fail. They are new every morning; great is My faithfulness.[7]

When I renew you, you will once again feel the warmth of fresh love, even though it will never be the same. But remember that expressions of love and responses to love will change. Love wears different faces. You wear different faces. Love sometimes says things differently, acts differently. It does not necessarily mean it is growing old or cold. It simply means there are changing seasons to love.

I do not change. My love is the same yesterday, today, and forever, even as I am the same yesterday, today, and forever.[8] But your responses to My love will reflect the ebb and flow of your life. Sometimes you will be exuberant, exhilarated, buoyant. Sometimes you will feel passion, awe, wonder. But you will not always ride the crest of high-emotion love. Sometimes you will feel solid, stable, on an even keel of contentment and enjoyment. Sometimes you will feel comfortable familiarity, or simple cordiality and good will.

Sometimes, you may not even feel at all, and no one will be able to see love written all over your face. It will not necessarily mean that love has cooled. It may simply mean that you need a good night's sleep or a walk in the woods or more vitamins and iron. Or it may mean that love is moving on to another phase.

Don't be afraid of stages. Don't be quick to assume that the changing responses to love in your life are setting you up for decline. The changes in how you respond to love may actually be setting you up for growth. Simply acknowledge the season through which your love is passing, give thanks for seasons of the past, and do not expect all seasons to look the same. "Forget the former things; do not dwell on the past. See, I am doing a new thing! Now it springs up; do you not perceive it? I am making a way in the desert and streams in the wasteland."[9]

When you have stopped trying to produce freshness on your own and have instead sunk your roots deep down to the silent spring of My love, freshness will return. Your thoughts will be of Me. You will not have to force them—they will come as easily and naturally as breathing. When your love is renewed, you cannot help but think about the loved one.

Renewed love naturally propagates itself. When your love is renewed, you will be "like a tree planted by streams of water, which yields its fruit in season and whose leaf does not wither."[10] When you feel loved, you will find yourself passing out love to others, as surely as an orange tree offers oranges to passersby. No tedious efforts to produce, no training programs required to grow fruit. So great will be your joy at being loved that you will not be able to contain yourself. Others will sense life in you. They will be refreshed by your fruit.

When you send your roots down to the silent spring, your leaf will not wither. You will be fresh, because you will constantly be fed. My love will be your daily supply, your never-ending reservoir.

When you are anchored in My love, you will talk to Me about more than the weather. You will want to tell Me about yourself. You will confide your sense of staleness, confess your fear of Ephesus, name your sadness over seasons past. In fact, you will be eager to talk, for you will sense how eager I am to listen. You will know that I'm not looking at My watch, tapping on the table, wondering how much longer this monologue will drag on. You will talk because you know you have My undivided attention. I hang on every word, watch your every expression. You will talk because you know I care about the details of your life — where you went, who you talked to, how you felt.

When the renewing waters of love start to flow afresh into your heart, you will want to be near Me. I will ask as I asked of My nation Israel, "Who is [she] who will devote [herself] to be close to me?"[11]

You will answer, "I do."

You will come, as did Mary of Bethany, to first sit at My feet and then to pour your pint of expensive perfume over them and wipe them with your hair, knowing that every act of devotion, no matter how humbly offered, will be lovingly accepted.[12]

Thaw your fear of the cold by remembering our past closeness. Recall how I said to you,

I have loved you with an everlasting love;
I have drawn you with loving-kindness. I
will build you up again and you will be
rebuilt, O Virgin Israel. Again you will
take up your tambourines and go out to
dance with the joyful. Again you will
plant vineyards on the hills of Samaria;
the farmers will plant them and enjoy their
fruit. . . . I will bring [you] from the land
of the north and gather [you] from the ends
of the earth. . . . [You] will pray as I bring
[you] back. I will lead [you] beside streams
of water on a level path where [you] will
not stumble. . . . I will watch over [you]
like a shepherd. . . . [You] will be like a
well-watered garden. . . . I will turn [your]
mourning into gladness; I will give [you]
comfort and joy instead of sorrow. I will
satisfy [you] with abundance, and [you]
will be filled with my bounty.[13]

When our love is fresh you will put away
your independence. You will be able to depend
on Me again, to ask for My help, to reach out for
My hand. You will realize that even as you and I
face storms together, our bond is strengthening.
As you learn to need Me again, you will become
strong—not in your independence, but in your
dependence on Me. You will realize anew that
"many waters cannot quench love; rivers cannot
wash it away."[14] You and I are in this together and
will be in it together as long as you are willing to
reach for My hand as you step into the waters.

When you are secure in My love, you can

let Me be your Savior in the midst of the waters. You will venture beyond the shallows out into the deep, for you will know, "When you pass through the waters, I will be with you; and when you pass through the rivers, they will not sweep over you."[15]

Come celebrate the living water that flows for you from an eternal spring. You need not fear stagnation. You need only draw nearer—put your roots down deep, settle in, and be at home in My love. Then every day will be a new day. Every day you will wonder at the richness of life that has come to you by My grace. Every day you will watch eagerly for My sunrise, search eagerly for My presence in the mundane activities of your world. Every day you will know Me better, and every day you will want to know Me more.

And every day you will live in joyful anticipation of My presence. You will think of My love for you as it is now, and as it will be on that day when I carry you across the threshold into the New Jerusalem—the home I am preparing for you.

Every day you will count the days until the wedding, when you and I will sit down together at the marriage supper of the Lamb. Then you will hear the proclamation for which your heart has been yearning:

> Now the dwelling of God is with men,
> and he will live with them. They will be
> his people, and God himself will be with
> them and be their God. He will wipe
> every tear from their eyes. There will be
> no more death or mourning or crying
> or pain, for the old order of things has

passed away. . . . I am making everything new! . . . I am the Alpha and the Omega, the Beginning and the End. To [her] who is thirsty I will give to drink without cost from the spring of the water of life. [She] who overcomes will inherit all this, and I will be [her] God and [she] will be my [daughter].[16]

On that day, child, I will call you by a new name. You will be a crown of splendor in My hand, a royal diadem in the hand of your God. I will delight in you, I will rejoice over you as a bridegroom rejoices over his bride.[17]

Come to the spring and drink deeply of My love. Let it flow over you, bringing a foretaste of that day when the river of life will flow for you through the New Jerusalem and love will be forever fresh.

Until then, turn from your fears and relax in My love. Here at the source you will find your renewal.

My watch indicates that it's time to return to the mundane. I breathe deeply of the fresh spring air; this time I notice its fragrance. I also notice how clear the lake is. No sludge or sand or silt. I walk past the men on the work crew, who are still cutting dead limbs and raking dry leaves. I pause, one last time, and reflect on the beauty of this place.

Somewhere, I think to myself, *an underground stream is doing its job.*

I am refreshed by the thought of a silent stream. I know one flows for me.

How could I ever doubt that I am loved?

I wait for You
in silent expectation.
I am ready
You are ready
ten minutes early;
You have come for me.

You take my hand.
We walk and talk —
about earthly memories
and heavenly plans.

You know the route
and gently lead me
up to the great gilded hall
through jasper that juts up against gold.
I catch my breath as we step through the arch:
trumpets sound,
candles glow,
crystal shines. . . .
Your table is set for me.

Then above me
I see the banners —
scripted in gold,
written by Your hand,
four letters:
L-O-V-E.
We sit down to dinner
under the biggest banner of them all.

You look at me
Your eyes are full of tears.
Finally, I am home
and I know I am loved.

NOTES
1. Revelation 2:4.
2. Matthew 24:12.
3. Psalm 119:11.
4. John 10:10.
5. Romans 6:4, 2 Corinthians 5:17.
6. Hebrews 8.
7. Lamentations 3:22-23.
8. Hebrews 13:8.
9. Isaiah 43:18-19.
10. Psalm 1:3.
11. Jeremiah 30:21.
12. John 12:1-7.
13. Jeremiah 31:3-14.
14. Song of Songs 8:17.
15. Isaiah 43:2.
16. Revelation 21:3-7.
17. Isaiah 62:2-5.